WATER

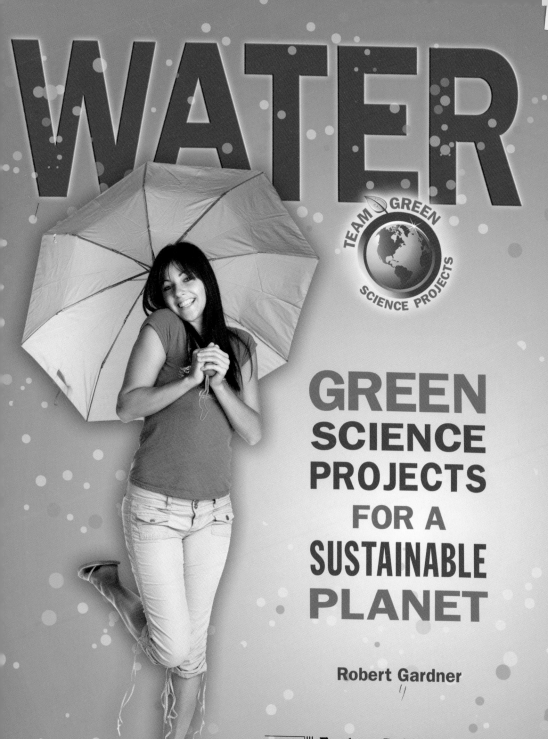

GREEN SCIENCE PROJECTS FOR A SUSTAINABLE PLANET

Robert Gardner

Enslow Publishers, Inc.
40 Industrial Road
Box 398
Berkeley Heights, NJ 07922
USA

http://www.enslow.com

WATER
GREEN Science Projects for a Sustainable PLANET

Library of Congress Cataloging-in-Publication Data

Gardner, Robert, 1929–
    Water : green science projects for a sustainable planet / Robert Gardner.
        p. cm. — (Team Green science projects)
    Includes bibliographical references and index.
    Summary: "Provides environmentally friendly 'green' science projects about water"—Provided
        by publisher.
    ISBN 978-0-7660-3645-1
    1. Hydrology—Juvenile literature. 2. Water—Experiments—Juvenile literature. 3. Science
        projects—Juvenile literature. I. Title.
    GB662.3.G37 2011
    551.48078—dc22

                                                           2009037902

Printed in the United States of America

102010 Lake Book Manufacturing, Inc., Melrose Park, IL

10 9 8 7 6 5 4 3 2 1

To Our Readers: We have done our best to make sure all Internet Addresses in this book were active and appropriate when we went to press. However, the author and the publisher have no control over and assume no liability for the material available on those Internet sites or on other Web sites they may link to. Any comments or suggestions can be sent by e-mail to comments@enslow.com or to the address on the back cover.

♻ Enslow Publishers, Inc., is committed to printing our books on recycled paper. The paper in every book contains 10% to 30% post-consumer waste (PCW). The cover board on the outside of each book contains 100% PCW. Our goal is to do our part to help young people and the environment too!

Illustration Credits: Bob Blaylock, p. 105 (d); Enslow Publishers, Inc., pp. 49, 63, 86; Hazel, Tracy E. The phlyogeny of the genus Brachiomonas. Bulletin of the Torrey Botanical Club. April, 1922, p. 105 (b); Stephen F. Delisle, pp. 35 (a, b), 91; Stephen Rountree (www.rountreegraphics.com), pp. 61, 67, 85, 98; Tom LaBaff, pp. 28, 30, 35 (c), 81, 90; Tom LaBaff and Stephanie LaBaff, pp. 26, 55, 65; Shutterstock.com, p. 105 (a, c, e, f); U.S. National Oceanic and Atmospheric Administration, p. 105 (g).

Photo Credits: Shutterstock.com

Cover Photo: Shutterstock.com

Contents

Introduction 7

    The Scientific Method 8

    Science Fairs 10

    Safety First 11

Chapter 1

Water, Water, Everywhere, But Little Left to Drink 12

  1.1 **Dividing Up Earth's Water (A Demonstration)** 14

  1.2 **Part of Your Virtual Water Footprint (An Analysis)** 22

Chapter 2

Water: A Compound Essential for Life 24

✅ 2.1 **An Effect of Water's Polarity (An Experiment)** 27

✅ 2.2 **Surface Tension: Another Effect of Water's Polarity (A Demonstration)** 29

✅ 2.3 **Surface Tension and Capillarity (An Experiment)** 33

  2.4 **Water, the Universal Solvent (An Experiment)** 37

✅ 2.5 **Boiling Water (An Experiment)** 41

✅ 2.6 **Melting Frozen Water (Ice) (A Demonstration)** 43

  2.7 **Volume Changes When Water Becomes a Gas (A Demonstration)** 46

✅ 2.8 **The Strange Behavior of Water When It Freezes (An Experiment)** 47

 Indicates experiments that offer ideas for science fair projects.

2.9 Heat Capacity and Specific Heat (An Experiment) 53

2.10 Comparing the Heat Capacities of Water and Sand
(A Demonstration) 58

Chapter 3

The Water Cycle 60

3.1 The Water Cycle: A Model 64

3.2 How Raindrops Are Made (An Experiment) 66

3.3 How Acidic Is Your Rain? (A Measurement) 69

3.4 A Model Aquifer 76

3.5 Pumping and Polluting an Aquifer (A Model) 80

3.6 Why Seawater and Freshwater Tend Not to Mix
(A Demonstration) 83

3.7 How Much Space Is There Between Soil Particles?
(A Measurement) 87

3.8 Transpiration (A Demonstration) 89

Chapter 4

Rivers, Lakes, Dams, Reservoirs,
and Wetlands 93

4.1 A Stream's Water Flow (A Measurement) 96

4.2 Aquatic Wetland Plants and Animals
(An Experiment) 104

Chapter 5

Conserving Water, a Precious Resource 107

5.1 Conserve Water, Don't Let It Leak Away
(A Measurement) 109

 Indicates experiments that offer ideas for science fair projects.

5.2 **Is the Water in Your Home Leaking Away?**
     (An Experiment) 110

✅ 5.3 **Conserve Water: Find the Leaks in Your Home**
     (Measurements) 112

✅ 5.4 **Bath or Shower? (An Experiment)** 114

Glossary 122

Appendix 124

Further Reading 125

Internet Addresses 126

Index 127

Introduction

Water is Earth's life-sustaining resource. Without this vital chemical compound, there would be no life. Water makes up two-thirds of the human body. It covers 70 percent of our planet. Yet most people realize the importance of water only when it is scarce. Droughts and the water rationing that accompany them bring it to our attention.

In this book, you will learn much about water and its significance. You will do so by reading, doing experiments to answer a question or test a hypothesis, making a model to illustrate an idea, or carrying out a demonstration to better understand a concept. You will see why the total mass of Earth's water does not change significantly. You will examine its unusual properties, follow its paths through the environment, discover the consequences of its excess or shortage, and learn how to conserve it.

At times, as you do the experiments, demonstrations, and other activities, you may need a partner to help you. It would be best to work with someone who enjoys experimenting as much as you do. In that way, you will both enjoy what you are doing. If any safety issues or danger is involved in doing an experiment, you will be warned. In some cases, to avoid danger, you will be asked to work with an adult. Please do so. We don't want you to take any chances that could lead to an injury.

Like any good scientist, you will find it useful to record your ideas, notes, data, and conclusions in a notebook. By doing so, you can keep track of the information you gather and the conclusions you reach. It will allow you to refer to things you have done, which will help you in doing future projects.

The Scientific Method

Scientists look at the world and try to understand how things work. They ask questions, make careful observations, and conduct research. Different areas of science use different approaches. Depending on the problem, one method is likely to be better than another. Designing a new medicine for heart disease, studying the spread of an invasive plant such as purple loosestrife, and finding evidence of water on Mars require different methods.

Despite the differences, all scientists use a similar general approach in doing experiments. It is called the scientific method. In most experiments, some or all of the following steps are used: making an observation, formulating a question, making a hypothesis (one possible answer to the question) and a prediction (an if-then statement), designing and conducting an experiment, analyzing results and drawing conclusions about your prediction, and accepting or rejecting the hypothesis. Scientists then share their findings by writing articles that are reviewed by other scientists before being published in journals.

You might wonder how to start an experiment. When you observe something in the world, you may become curious and ask a question. Your question, which could arise from an earlier experiment or from reading, may be answered by a well-designed investigation. Once you have a question, you can make a hypothesis. Your hypothesis is a possible answer to the question (what you think will happen). Once you have a hypothesis, it is time to design an experiment to test your hypothesis.

In most cases, it is appropriate to do a controlled experiment. This means having two groups that are treated exactly the same except for the single factor being tested. That factor is often called a variable. For example, suppose this is your question: "Is water less dense than cooking oil?" You might use a balance and a graduated cylinder. You could weigh 100 mL of water and then weigh an equal volume of cooking oil at the same temperature as the water. During the experiment, you would collect data. You would observe and record the mass and volume of each liquid. You would then divide the mass of each liquid by its volume. By comparing the quotients, you would be able to draw a conclusion.

Two other terms are often used in scientific experiments: *dependent* and *independent* variables. The dependent variable depends on the value of the independent variable. Here, the dependent value is the mass of the liquids. It depends on the volume, the independent variable in this experiment. After the data is collected, it is analyzed to see if it supports or rejects the hypothesis. The results of one experiment often lead you to a related question. Or they may send you off in a different direction. Whatever the results, something can be learned from every experiment.

9

Science Fairs

Some of the experiments in this book contain ideas you might use at a science fair. Those projects are indicated with a symbol (☑). However, judges at science fairs do not reward projects or experiments that are simply copied from a book. For example, a diagram or model of a water molecule would not impress most judges; however, a unique way to measure water's surface tension or reduce the use of water would be more likely to attract their attention.

Science fair judges tend to reward creative thought and imagination. It is difficult to be creative or imaginative unless you are really interested in your project. Therefore, try to choose an investigation that excites you. And before you jump into a project, consider, too, your own talents and the cost of the materials you will need.

If you decide to use an experiment or idea found in this book for a science fair, find ways to modify or extend it. This should not be difficult. As you carry out investigations, new ideas will come to mind. You will think of questions that experiments can answer. The experiments will make excellent science fair projects, particularly because the ideas are your own and are interesting to you.

If you decide to enter a science fair and have never done so, read some of the books listed in the Further Reading section. These books deal specifically with science fairs. They provide plenty of helpful hints and useful information. The books will help you avoid the pitfalls that sometimes plague first-time entrants. You will learn how to prepare appealing reports that include charts and graphs, how to set up and display your work, how to present your project, and how to relate to judges and visitors.

Safety First

As with many activities, safety is important in science. Certain rules apply when doing experiments. Some of the rules below may seem obvious to you, others may not, but it is important that you follow all of them.

1. Have **an adult** help you whenever the book advises.

2. Wear eye protection and closed-toe shoes (not sandals). Tie back long hair.

3. Do not eat or drink while experimenting. Never taste substances being used (unless instructed to do so).

4. Do not touch chemicals.

5. The liquid in some thermometers is mercury (a dense liquid metal). It is dangerous to touch mercury or breathe mercury vapor, and such thermometers have been banned in many states. When doing these experiments, use only non-mercury thermometers, such as those filled with alcohol. If you have a mercury thermometer in the house, **ask an adult** if it can be taken to a local thermometer exchange location.

6. Do only those experiments that are described in the book or those that have been approved by **an adult**.

7. Maintain a serious attitude while conducting experiments. Never engage in horseplay or play practical jokes.

8. Before beginning an experiment, read all the instructions carefully and be sure you understand them.

9. Remove all items not needed for the experiment from your work space.

10. At the end of every activity, clean all materials used and put them away. Then wash your hands thoroughly with soap and water.

Water, Water, Everywhere, But Little Left to Drink

Seventy percent of Earth's volume, 1.09 trillion cubic kilometers (260 billion cubic miles), is covered by a vast amount of water—1.37 billion cubic kilometers (328 million cubic miles) of it. However, nearly 97 percent of that water (1.32 billion cubic kilometers or 317 million cubic miles) is in our oceans, which are about 3.5 percent salt. Humans cannot drink seawater. The salt concentration in our body fluids is much less than 3.5 percent. Seawater will "pull" water out of our bodies. It will cause our bodies to dehydrate. The living cells of many of the plants we grow for food have about the same salt concentration as human cells. Consequently, these plants cannot grow in salt water or soil that is salty.

Freshwater makes up only 46 million cubic kilometers (11 million cubic miles), which is 3 percent of Earth's water. Most of it exists as ice near Earth's poles. Table 1 reveals where Earth's water is found.

Table 1:
The location and quantity of Earth's water.

Location	Quantity (cubic kilometers)	Quantity (cubic miles)	Percentage of Earth's Water
Oceans (salt water)	1,320,000,000	317,000,000	96.6
Polar regions (ice)	37,530,000	9,000,000	2.7
Underground and available	4,170,000	1,000,000	0.3
Underground and unavailable	4,170,000	1,000,000	0.3
Lakes and ponds	125,000	30,000	0.009
Soil	66,700	16,000	0.005
Atmosphere	12,900	3,100	0.0009
Rivers	1,250	300	0.00009
TOTAL	1,367,000,000	328,000,000	100

1.1 Dividing Up Earth's Water (A Demonstration)

The way that Earth's water is distributed is shown in Table 1. By doing this demonstration, you can get a better sense of how the total volume of Earth's water is divided. You will separate a much smaller volume into the same fractional parts shown in Table 1.

Things YOU will Need:

- ✓ metric measuring cup or 1-liter soda bottle
- ✓ pail or dishpan
- ✓ eyedropper
- ✓ graduated medicine cup
- ✓ cup
- ✓ 5 medicine cups, vials, or small paper cups
- ✓ saucers
- ✓ wooden toothpick
- ✓ plastic wrap or waxed paper

1. Add 4 liters (4,000 mL) of water to a pail or dishpan. Let this amount of water represent all of the world's water.

2. Using a graduated medicine cup and eyedropper, remove 108 mL of water from the 4.0 liters. Put that water into a cup. That volume represents the frozen water near Earth's poles.

3. Using an eyedropper and a graduated medicine cup, remove 24 mL of water from the pail or dishpan. Put it in another

medicine cup or vial. That water represents the water under the ground. Only half of it (12 mL) is available for human use.

4. Again, use the eyedropper to remove 7 drops from the pail or dishpan. Place those drops in another medicine cup or vial. The 7 drops represent the water in Earth's lakes and ponds.

5. Remove 4 drops of water from the pail or dishpan. Put the 4 drops of water in another medicine cup or vial. Those 4 drops represent the water in Earth's soil.

6. Remove one drop of water from the pail or dishpan. Put that drop in another medicine cup or vial. It represents slightly more than all the water in Earth's atmosphere.

7. Finally, dip the narrow tip of a wooden toothpick into the pail or dishpan of water. Remove the toothpick and tap it on a piece of plastic wrap or waxed paper. That amount of water—about 1/10th of a drop—represents the water in Earth's rivers.

8. The water remaining in the pail or dishpan (about 3,864 mL) represents the water in Earth's oceans.

FACT

Roughly 16 billion tons of rain falls on the United States during an average day. One trillion tons of rain falls on Earth each day. That much rain, if collected, would occupy more than 200 cubic miles or about 7 percent of the water in the atmosphere. However, approximately the same quantity of water evaporates into the atmosphere. As a result, the concentration of water in the atmosphere remains constant.

Where Our Water Is Used

Table 2 shows where most water is used on a daily basis in the United States. It also reveals how much of that water is consumed (not returned to its source). Electric power plants, for example, return most of the water used to generate electricity. Much of the water used to irrigate crops evaporates.

Table 2:
Where water is used and consumed in the United States.

User	Water Used (liters/day)*	Water Consumed (liters/day)**
Electric power plants	600 billion	20 billion
Agricultural irrigation	570 billion	310 billion
Industries	170 billion	20 billion
Domestic	150 billion	40 billion

* To convert to gallons, multiply by 0.26.

** Consumed water means it is not returned to its source.

Hydroelectric power plants use moving water in rivers or from dams to generate electricity. These power plants use about 10 percent of the 600 billion liters (158 billion gallons) of water shown in Table 2. The remaining 90 percent is used by thermoelectric plants. In these plants, water is heated to steam, which turns the giant turbines used to generate electrical energy. Water is also used to cool the steam.

Industries that use large amounts of water include those that manufacture paper, chemicals, plastics, petroleum, steel, and other metals. Most of these industries now recycle water, which is why they consume so much less than agriculture.

Increased conservation of water can significantly reduce domestic use of water. In later chapters, you will see how households can reduce their water consumption.

In the United States, only 5 percent of agricultural land is irrigated. However, irrigated land produces 20 percent of our crops. As Table 2 shows, however, irrigation is not an efficient process. In Israel, where water is precious, deserts have been changed to green fields by using drip irrigation to water crops. Narrow pipes buried in the soil deliver water directly to the roots of plants. This method of irrigation prevents the huge water losses caused by evaporation when ditches or sprinklers are used to irrigate.

A growing world population requires ever more food. To meet this demand, agriculture must use our limited water more efficiently. Drip irrigation can help us meet that requirement. Progress can also be made in other ways. Geneticists are developing plants that require less water, are more resistant to disease and drought, and produce more fruit. In the United States, people are being encouraged to eat fruits, vegetables, fish, and poultry rather than beef, pork, lamb, and other fatty foods. Such changes in dietary habits can help to conserve water because growing these foods requires less water and growing area to produce.

Water is usually measured by volume, but there are different ways to measure volume. Some of the most common ones used to measure water are shown in Table 3.

Small volumes can be measured in milliliters (mL) or ounces (oz). Larger volumes are measured in liters (L), quarts (qt), or gallons (gal). Still larger volumes can be measured in cubic feet, cubic yards, or cubic meters (m^3). Very large volumes, such as those in Table 1, are measured in cubic kilometers or cubic miles.

Table 3:
Metric and U.S. Customary units of volume and their equivalents.

Metric	U.S. Customary	Converting Between Metric and U.S. Customary
1,000 mL = 1.0 L	32 oz = 1.0 qt	1.0 oz = 29.5 mL
1.0 m^3 = 1,000 L	4 qt = 1 gal	1 qt = 0.946 L
1.0 km^3 = 1,000,000,000 m^3	1 ft^3 = 7.48 gal	1 gal = 3.78 L
	1 mi^3 = 147 billion ft^3	1 mi^3 = 4.17 km^3
	1 mi^3 = 19.7 billion gal	

Virtual Water

The quantity of water needed to produce a product is called virtual water. For example, it takes about 1,000 kilograms (2,200 pounds) or liters of water to make one kilogram (2.2 pounds) of wheat you can eat. In a sense, each kilogram of wheat holds 1,000 kilograms of

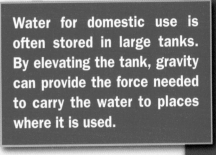

Water for domestic use is often stored in large tanks. By elevating the tank, gravity can provide the force needed to carry the water to places where it is used.

water—the water required to turn the wheat seeds into a kilogram of wheat.

It makes sense for dry regions to make use of virtual water by importing crops that require lots of water to grow. They can then use their limited water for other purposes. For example, suppose a kilogram of wheat is produced in a country where water is not scarce. If that wheat is eaten by people in another country, which is arid, this arid country did not need to use 1,000 kg of water to produce the wheat. It could instead use that water for drinking or other purposes.

Southern China, which has plentiful water, can grow rice. Some of that rice can be shipped to arid regions in northern China. Northern China can then use its limited water for drinking and sanitation. The nation of Jordan conserves about two-thirds of its water by importing foods with a high virtual water content.

Agriculture accounts for nearly 80 percent of the world's use of water. Drinking and bathing account for much less. Because the United States is a food exporter, it is also an exporter of virtual water. Other countries that are water exporters include Canada, Australia, Argentina, and Thailand. Virtual water importers include Japan, Sri Lanka, and Italy. As the world population grows and global warming changes climates, many more countries will be faced with water shortages. Methods for conserving water will become increasingly important.

The amount of water a person uses in a year is his or her annual virtual water footprint. The footprint includes all the water used to produce the food he or she eats, clothes he or she wears, and the use of other products that require water to make. The footprint of the average American citizen (2.5 million L/yr, or 656,000 gal/yr) is twice that of the average world citizen (1.24 million liters, or 328,000 gallons). In China, that yearly footprint is only 700,000 L/yr, or 185,000 gal/yr; in Japan it is 1.15 million L/yr, or 300,000 gal/yr.

As you can see from Table 4, which shows the virtual water for some common foods, it takes less water to grow fruits and vegetables than to grow meat. It takes several years for animals to mature; fruits and vegetables are harvested annually. A vegetarian, therefore, usually has a smaller virtual water foot-print than someone who eats meat. The virtual water consumed per day by the average American vegetarian is about 3,780 liters (1,000 gallons). A meat eater consumes about 40 percent more.

Table 4:
The virtual water needed to produce various foods.

Product	Virtual Water Needed		Product	Virtual Water Needed	
	liters	gallons		liters	gallons
1 pound of wheat	605	160	1 cup of coffee	140	37
1 apple	72	19	1 banana	102	27
1 slice of bread	38	10	1 sheet of paper	11	3
1 orange	49	13	1 pound of corn	408	108
1 pound of chicken	1,777	468	1 pound of beef	7,182	1,897
1 pound of rice	1,550	409	1 pound of lamb	2,174	574
1 pound of cheese	2,268	599	1 glass of milk	238	63
1 pound of potatoes	284	75	1 pound of green beans	816	216
1 hamburger	2,419	639	1 glass of orange juice	227	60
1 egg	246	65	1 pound of chicken	1,285	339
1 pound of rice	2,722	719	1 pound of pork	2,684	709

1.2 Part of Your Virtual Water Footprint

(An Analysis)

Things **YOU** will **Need:** ✓ Table 4

Food for two lunches, A and B, are listed below.

Lunch A	Lunch B
1 cup of coffee	1 glass of milk
1 hamburger	1 chicken sandwich (2 slices of bread + 4 ounces of chicken)
potatoes (4 ounces)	
1 ounce of wheat crackers	4 ounces of green beans
1 hard-boiled egg	1 hard-boiled egg
2 bananas	1 orange

How much virtual water, in gallons, was needed for each lunch? How much virtual water, in liters, was needed for each lunch?

You can live a *greener* life and reduce your food budget as well as your contribution to global warming by eating fewer meat and dairy products. Meat costs more per pound than other protein sources such as tofu and beans. And livestock waste, which pollutes water also generates methane, a potent greenhouse gas. When and if you do eat meat or dairy products, choose those from grass-fed animals. Less fertilizer and pesticides, which can pollute water, are used for grasses than for grains.

There are lots of experiments with water that relate to conservation, pollution, and the environment that you will do in later chapters. But first, in Chapter 2, you will investigate some of the properties of this amazing compound that is essential to life.

Water:

A Compound

Essential for Life

For most Americans, water is readily available. Turn the handle of a faucet and out it pours. Drink a glassful and it quenches your thirst. Add a bit of soap and it cleans your body. Pour it onto a variety of other substances and those substances disappear. They disappear because they dissolve—their parts are spread uniformly throughout the water. Water is known as the universal solvent because so many substances—solids, liquids, and gases—will dissolve in it. Because minerals dissolve in water, they are made available to microscopic plants and animals that form the base of aquatic food webs. However, many pollutants, such as sewage, nitrogen- and phosphorus-rich fertilizers, and toxic chemicals, are also water soluble. As a result, our water sources are often polluted.

Figure 1

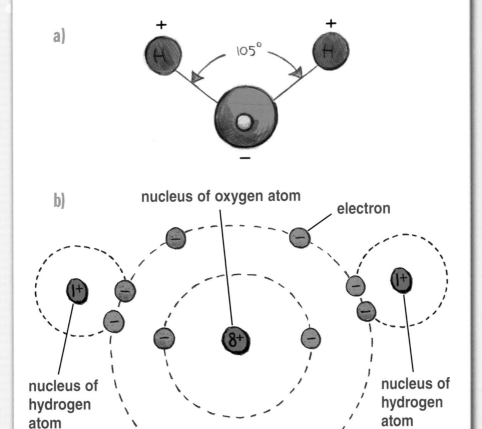

a) In a water molecule, H_2O, the hydrogen atoms are at an angle of 105 degrees.

b) Oxygen attracts the ten electrons more strongly than do the two hydrogen atoms.

Because water is so common, we tend to take it for granted. We give it little thought. But, as you will see, water has some very uncommon properties. These properties are the result of the unique nature of the molecules that make up water. As you probably know, water is called "H-two-O," which chemically translates to H_2O. This chemical formula shows that a water molecule is made up of two atoms of hydrogen and one atom of oxygen. Because of the internal structure of oxygen atoms, the two hydrogen atoms are not connected to the oxygen atom at an angle of 180 degrees. Rather, they are separated by 105 degrees, as shown in Figure 1a. This angle between the hydrogen atoms causes parts of a water molecule to have different amounts of charge. The oxygen atom attracts the molecule's 10 negatively charged electrons (Figure 1b) more strongly than do the two hydrogen atoms. As a result, the oxygen end of the molecule has a slight negative charge. The hydrogen ends of the molecule are slightly positive. Because one side of the molecule is positive and the other side negative, the molecule is said to be polar. You can see that water molecules are polar by doing an experiment.

2.1 An Effect of Water's Polarity
(An Experiment)

Things YOU will Need:
- ✓ plastic comb
- ✓ woolen cloth
- ✓ kitchen sink and faucet
- ✓ nail
- ✓ foam cup
- ✓ cooking oil
- ✓ bowl

Hypothesis: Water molecules are polar; therefore, they will be affected by an electric charge.

1. Rub a plastic comb briskly with a woolen cloth. This will put an electric charge on the comb.

2. Hold the comb near a very thin stream of water flowing from a kitchen faucet (Figure 2). What happens to the stream of water? What evidence do you have that water molecules are polar? Was the hypothesis correct?

Hypothesis: Cooking oil molecules may not be polar. If they are not polar, they will not be attracted to an electric charge.

3. Repeat the experiment with a thin stream of cooking oil. Use a nail to make a small hole in the bottom of a foam cup.

4. Hold the cup over a bowl in the sink. Add cooking oil to the cup so that a thin stream of oil flows out of the cup into

Figure 2

An experiment can show if water molecules are polar.

the bowl. Bring the charged comb near the stream. What evidence do you have that cooking oil molecules are not polar? Was the hypothesis correct?

Idea for a Science Fair Project

Design and carry out an experiment to identify the charge (+ or –) on various objects rubbed with a variety of cloths (silk, wool, cotton, nylon) and papers (towels, newspaper, facial tissue).

2.2 Surface Tension: Another Effect of Water's Polarity

(A Demonstration)

Things **YOU** will **Need:**

- ✓ cold tap water
- ✓ clean bowl
- ✓ clean dinner fork
- ✓ paper clip
- ✓ clean plastic vial or medicine cup
- ✓ eyedropper
- ✓ waxed paper
- ✓ toothpick
- ✓ light cooking oil
- ✓ tall, clear glass
- ✓ ice cube

Because water molecules are polar, they attract one another. There is an attractive (cohesive) force pulling them together. For a water molecule surrounded by liquid water, the forces on it are equal in all directions. But for surface molecules, the forces are directed inward toward molecules below the surface and toward other surface molecules (see Figure 3). The inward force on the surface molecules pulls them together. This gives the surface of water a skin-like quality, a property referred to as surface tension. To see that water really does have a skinlike quality, do the following steps.

Figure 3

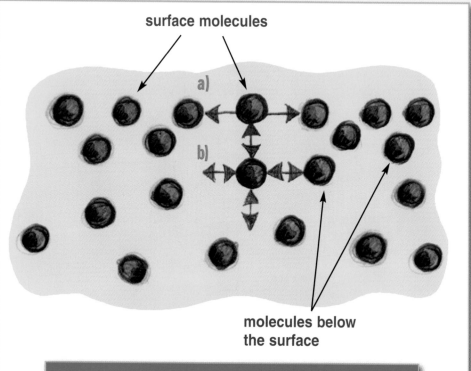

surface molecules

molecules below
the surface

3 a) Molecules on the surface of the water are attracted
by molecules within the liquid (beneath the surface)
and by other surface molecules.
b) Molecules of water within the liquid are attracted
equally in all directions.

1. Nearly fill a clean bowl with cold tap water.

2. Using a clean dinner fork, gently place a paper clip on the surface of the water in the bowl. Notice that the paper clip doesn't sink. Look closely. You will see that the paper clip bends the water's "skin."

3. To see another effect of water's surface tension, fill a clean plastic vial or medicine cup to the brim with cold tap water.

4. Using an eyedropper, see how high you can heap the water above the edge of the vial or medicine cup. Notice how water's skin allows it to heap well above the rim.

5. Examine another effect of the attraction between water molecules. Using a clean eyedropper, place a drop of water on a sheet of waxed paper. Look at the drop from its side. Notice its round shape. Place a second drop of water near the first one. Then use a toothpick to slowly move the second drop closer to the first one. What happens when the two drops touch?

Surface tension prevents this paper clip from sinking.

6. Add light cooking oil to a tall, clear glass until it is about two-thirds full. Place an ice cube in the cooking oil. (What does the fact that it floats tell you?) Watch closely as a drop of meltwater forms at the base of the ice cube. What shape does the drop have? How can you explain its shape?

Ideas for a Science Fair Project

- Repeat Experiment 2.2 using alcohol, cooking oil, and soapy water in place of water. How might you expect the results to differ? How do they differ?

- Design and carry out an experiment to measure the surface tension of different liquids.

2.3 Surface Tension and Capillarity
(An Experiment)

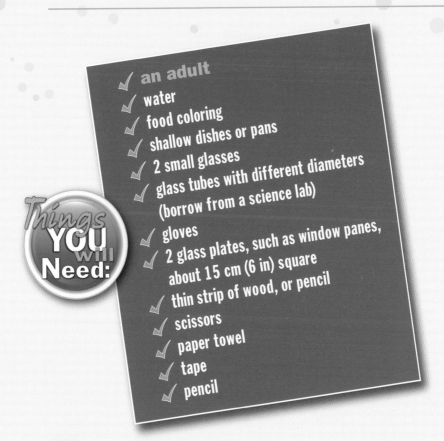

Things YOU will Need:

- ✓ an adult
- ✓ water
- ✓ food coloring
- ✓ shallow dishes or pans
- ✓ 2 small glasses
- ✓ glass tubes with different diameters (borrow from a science lab)
- ✓ gloves
- ✓ 2 glass plates, such as window panes, about 15 cm (6 in) square
- ✓ thin strip of wood, or pencil
- ✓ scissors
- ✓ paper towel
- ✓ tape
- ✓ pencil

Water adheres (sticks) to glass and other solids because there is an attraction between water molecules and the molecules of the solids. You also know that water holds together very well.

Hypothesis: Because water holds together very well and adheres to glass and many other substances it will "climb up" glass tubes and other surfaces. To test this hypothesis, you can do an experiment.

1. Add some water and a few drops of food coloring to a shallow dish.

2. Invert two small drinking glasses and place them in the colored water.

3. Move the sides of the glasses very close together, as shown in Figure 4a. What happens to the water in the narrow space between the glass surfaces?

4. If possible, borrow some glass tubes with different diameters from a science lab. Place the tubes in some colored water. How does the diameter of the hollow tube affect the height to which the water rises?

5. **Put on gloves and do this part of the experiment with an adult.** Find two glass plates, such as window-panes, that are about 15 cm (6 in) square. Fasten one end of the plates with tape, as shown in Figure 4b. Place a thin strip of wood or a pencil between the plates at the other end. Tape that end as shown. Put the glass plates in a shallow dish that holds colored water. How is the height of the water between the plates related to the distance the plates are separated?

   There are tiny spaces between the wood fibers in paper towels. Will water "climb up" paper towels?

6. To find out, cut a strip about 2.5 cm (1 in) wide from a paper towel. Tape the top of the strip to a pencil so that it hangs vertically. Dip the lower end of the towel into a drinking glass with a small amount of colored water (see Figure 4c). Does water "climb" the towel? Was the hypothesis correct?

   The tendency of water and other polar liquids to "climb up" narrow tubes and spaces is called *capillarity*.

Figure 4

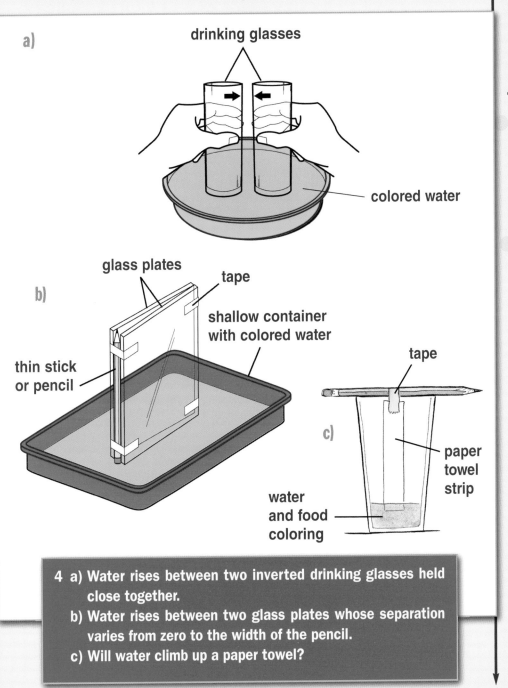

a)

drinking glasses

colored water

b)

glass plates

tape

shallow container with colored water

thin stick or pencil

tape

c)

paper towel strip

water and food coloring

4 a) Water rises between two inverted drinking glasses held close together.
b) Water rises between two glass plates whose separation varies from zero to the width of the pencil.
c) Will water climb up a paper towel?

Ideas for a Science Fair Project

- Design and carry out an experiment to show that the height that water rises in a tube is inversely proportional to the diameter of the tube. In other words, show that doubling the diameter halves the height of the water, tripling the diameter reduces the height to a third, and so on.

- Cut long strips of paper towels that differ in width. Does the width of the strip affect the height to which water will rise within the towel? If it does, how can you explain what you observe?

- Find a way to enclose the paper towel strips. You might use long, wide plastic tubes or make covers from plastic wrap or waxed paper. How does enclosing the strips affect the height to which the water will rise? Can you explain what you observe?

Capillarity and Trees

Capillarity is one way groundwater reaches the roots of plants. Water adheres to many types of soil particles. The narrow spaces between the soil particles causes water deep within soil to move up to where it can be absorbed by the roots of plants.

Capillarity is also involved in the upward movement of water inside plants. Water evaporates from the leaves of plants, including tall trees. The evaporation creates tension in the tiny water-filled tubes that extend from a tree's roots to its leaves.

2.4 Water, the Universal Solvent
(A Demonstration)

If a solid dissolves (disappears) when mixed with a liquid, we say the solid is *soluble* in the liquid. The solid that dissolves is called the *solute*. The liquid in which it dissolves is called the *solvent*.

If little or none of the solid dissolves, the solute is *insoluble*. In general, substances that are not polar, such as gasoline and waxes, are not soluble in water. Polar substances tend to be soluble in water. Many polar chemical compounds are ionic. Ionic compounds are made up of atoms that carry an electric charge. For example, ordinary salt, sodium chloride (NaCl), contains sodium ions (Na^+), which have a positive charge, and chloride ions (Cl^-), which have a negative charge. The general properties of polar and nonpolar compounds are listed in Table 5.

Table 5:
General properties of polar and nonpolar compounds.

Type of Compound	General Properties
Polar	Ends of molecules carry a small electric charge opposite in sign. Polar substances may be ionic. If ionic, the compound exists as positive and negative ions (atoms carrying a + or − charge). Tend to form ions in water. Tend to be soluble in other polar compounds. Tend to be insoluble in nonpolar compounds.
Nonpolar	Molecules are uniformly neutral, not ionic. Do not form ions in water. Tend to be soluble in other nonpolar compounds. Tend to be insoluble in polar compounds.

As you know, salt—sodium chloride (NaCl)—is a solid that consists of sodium ions (Na^+) and chloride ions (Cl^-).

Hypothesis: Because salt consists of charged atoms (ions), it will dissolve in water's polar molecules.

To test this hypothesis:

1. Add one teaspoon of salt to a small glass. Nearly fill the glass with water and stir the mixture. Does salt dissolve in water?

   As you found in Experiment 2.1, cooking oil appears to be nonpolar. Would you expect cooking oil to dissolve in water? What is your hypothesis?

2. To find out, add one teaspoon of cooking oil to a small glass filled with water. Stir the two liquids. Does cooking oil dissolve in water? Was your hypothesis correct?

3. Try dissolving the following substances in water: sugar, baking soda, baking powder, starch, flour, vinegar, Kool-Aid™ drink mix crystals, and alcohol. Which substances do you think consist of polar molecules or ions? Which do you think consist of nonpolar molecules?

4. Dissolve some salt in water. Pour some of the solution onto a saucer. Leave the saucer uncovered in a place where it will not be disturbed. Examine the saucer for several days. What happens?

Just for Fun

A suspension is a mixture that contains small particles of an insoluble solid dispersed through a liquid. You can make a very interesting suspension by putting 125 mL (1/2 cup) of cornstarch into a bowl and adding half as much water. Mix the solid and liquid together with your hands. What happens when you try to squeeze a handful of the stuff? Try to pick up the mixture using a spoon. Put some of the suspension on a flat surface. What happens to it? Punch a small hole in a piece of paper and put some of the mixture over the hole. Does it leak through? What other properties do you notice about this strange stuff?

Salty Soil

As you saw in Experiment 2.4, when the water evaporates from a salt solution, it leaves the salt behind. All water, even freshwater, has some dissolved salt.

When early civilizations spread eastward from Egypt to Iraq, Iran, Pakistan, India, and China, the farmers used river water to irrigate their crops. But over time, as water evaporated and left salt behind, the soils became salty and less productive. In Egypt, land irrigated by the Nile River remained fertile. Each year that river flooded, bringing fresh soil to the land and washing salts in the old soil into the Mediterranean Sea.

In California, where irrigation provides the United States with 40 percent of its fresh fruits and vege-tables, four acre-feet* of water are required for each acre of the soil on which crops are grown. Where water can drain away from the soil and eventually be carried to an ocean, the salt can be removed from the soil. But in soil that cannot be drained, salt will accumulate and eventually the soil will be too salty for crops to grow. Water on irrigated land in California's Imperial and Coachella valleys drains into the Salton Sea. That sea is more than 60 meters (200 ft) below sea level. Soil drainage into the Salton Sea has made it saltier than the oceans.

* An acre-foot of water is enough water to cover an acre of land with water 1/3 meter (one foot) deep. That requires 43,560 cubic feet (325,851 gallons, 1,233,480 liters) of water.

2.5 **Boiling Water**
(An Experiment)

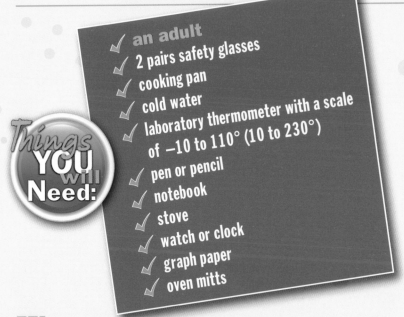

Things YOU will Need:

- ✓ an adult
- ✓ 2 pairs safety glasses
- ✓ cooking pan
- ✓ cold water
- ✓ laboratory thermometer with a scale of −10 to 110° (10 to 230°)
- ✓ pen or pencil
- ✓ notebook
- ✓ stove
- ✓ watch or clock
- ✓ graph paper
- ✓ oven mitts

Work with an adult on this experiment. You should both wear safety glasses and oven mitts.

Hypothesis: The temperature at which water boils can be determined by doing the following steps.

1. Half fill a cooking pan with cold water. Put a laboratory thermometer with a scale of −10 to 110°C (10 to 230°F) in the water. Record the temperature of the cold water in your notebook.

2. Put the pan of water with the thermometer on the heating element of a stove. Heat the water. Do not let the bulb of the thermometer touch the pan.

3. As the water warms, record the water temperature at one-minute intervals.

4. Notice the small bubbles that form and rise to the surface. Some are bubbles of air that were dissolved in the water. You have probably seen such air bubbles in a cold glass of water that has warmed. But other bubbles form when liquid water changes to gas. When the water begins to boil vigorously, the gaseous water bubbles rise to the surface and burst. What is the temperature of boiling water?

5. Continue heating the water and recording its temperature until about half of it has boiled away (changed to a gas). According to your measurements, what is the boiling temperature of water? Was the hypothesis correct?

    Use your data to plot a temperature vs. time graph. How can you account for the shape of the graph?

Ideas for a Science Fair Project

- People living in Denver, Colorado, say that water there boils at about 95°C (203°F). Can this be true? If it is true, how can it be explained?

- Design and do an experiment to determine how much heat is needed to change one gram of liquid water to gaseous water.

2.6 Melting Frozen Water (Ice)

(A Demonstration)

We know the actual mass of a water molecule. It is 2.99×10^{-23} gram, or 0.0000000000000000000000299 g, or 2.99 g divided by 100 billion trillion.

Long before scientists knew the actual masses of atoms and molecules, they knew their masses relative to oxygen. They assumed oxygen atoms weighed 16 atomic mass units (amu). They chose oxygen to be 16 because it was 16 times as heavy as hydrogen, the lightest element. By choosing oxygen as 16 amu, they avoided fractions. They knew hydrogen was 1/16th as heavy as oxygen so a hydrogen atom must weigh 1.0 amu, 1/16th that of an oxygen atom.

Because water molecules are strongly attracted to one another, they must acquire significant kinetic (motion) energy to separate into a gas. Their strong attraction for one another can be seen by comparing boiling temperatures for compounds and elements that have molecular masses similar to water.

Temperature, as you may know, is a measure of the kinetic (motion) energy of molecules. The faster molecules move, the higher their temperature. Table 6 lists the boiling points of some elements and compounds that have molecular weights comparable to water. As you can see, water has an unusually high boiling point (temperature) when compared to substances with equal or even higher molecular mass.

In Table 6, there is a question mark for the melting point of water. Based on what you know about water molecules, how would you expect its melting point to compare with other molecules of similar mass?

To check your prediction, do the following demonstration.

1. Nearly fill a pint-size plastic container with crushed ice or snow. (Snow consists of solid crystals of water.)

2. Put a thermometer into the crushed ice or snow and stir. In your notebook, record the temperature at one-minute intervals. While the ice is melting, what do you notice about the temperature? What is the meting point of solid water? Does it agree with your prediction?

3. Repeat the experiment with larger and smaller quantities of crushed ice or snow. Does the melting point depend on the amount of ice or snow?

Idea for a Science Fair Project

How would you expect the freezing temperature of water to compare with its melting temperature? Design and do an experiment to find out if you are right.

Table 6:

Molecular masses, boiling points, and melting points of a number of different elements and compounds.

Substance	Molecular Mass (amu)	Boiling Point (°C)	Melting Point (°C)
water (H_2O)	18	100	?
ammonia (NH_3)	17	−33.3	−77.7
bromine (Br_2)	159.8	58.8	−7.2
chlorine (Cl_2)	71	−34	−101
fluorine (F_2)	38	−188	−219.6
hydrogen chloride (HCl)	36.5	−84.9	−114.2
hydrogen sulfide (H_2S)	34.1	−60.2	−82.3
nitric oxide (NO)	30	−150.8	−163.6
nitrogen (N_2)	28	−195.8	−210

2.7 Volume Changes When Water Becomes a Gas
(A Demonstration)

Things **YOU** will **Need:**

- ✓ an adult
- ✓ ice cube
- ✓ one-gallon, clear plastic bag that can be sealed
- ✓ microwave oven
- ✓ clock or watch with second hand
- ✓ oven mitt

1. Put an ice cube into a one-gallon, clear plastic bag that can be sealed. Get all the air out of the bag by flattening it. Then seal the bag so that nothing can get in or out.

2. Place the bag in a microwave oven. Have an adult turn on the oven for 20 seconds at a time at maximum power. Watch what happens through the window.

   How much time is needed to melt the ice? How much time passes before the water begins to boil? What happens to the volume as the water boils and becomes a gas?

3. The adult should stop heating when the bag is nearly full with gas. Keep the oven closed for several minutes. What happens as the gas cools?

4. Ask an adult wearing an oven mitt to remove the bag of HOT water.

2.8 The Strange Behavior of Water When It Freezes

(An Experiment)

Things
YOU
will
Need:

✓ ice cube
✓ drinking glass
✓ water
✓ food coloring
✓ clay
✓ small jar
✓ transparent plastic drinking straw
✓ marking pen
✓ freezer
✓ clock or watch

$\mathbf{A}$s you saw in the previous experiment, the volume of a gas was much larger than that of the liquid from which it came. In fact, the volume occupied by a gas is about a thousand times greater than its liquid volume. This is because, on average, the molecules of a gas are about ten times farther apart than they are in a liquid.

When a liquid freezes, the volume of the solid is usually smaller than the volume of the liquid that froze. Most substances contract as they change from liquid to solid. In general, the density of a substance increases as its temperature decreases. The change in density is greatest when a gas condenses to a liquid, but there is usually also an increase in density when a liquid freezes to become a solid.

1. To see why the behavior of water is strangely different, put an ice cube in a glass of water. Does the ice sink or float? What does this tell you about the comparative density of solid and liquid water?

Hypothesis: Because ice is less dense than water, the volume will increase when water freezes.

2. Test the hypothesis by doing an experiment. Add several drops of food coloring to a glass of water.

3. Place a lump of clay in a small jar.

4. Put a transparent plastic drinking straw in the water and stir. Then place your finger firmly on the top of the immersed straw as shown in Figure 5a. By keeping your finger on the top of the straw, the water will remain in the straw when you lift it out of the glass.

5. Keeping your finger on the top of the straw, carry the straw and water to the jar with the lump of clay. Press the bottom of the straw into the clay. When you remove your finger from the straw, the water should remain in place (Figure 5b).

6. When you are convinced that water is not leaking from the straw, mark the water level in the straw with a marking pen. Place the jar that holds the clay and water-filled straw in a freezer. After about an hour, open the freezer and look at the water level in the straw. Has the water turned to ice? What happened to the volume as the liquid water changed to solid ice? Was the hypothesis correct?

Figure 5

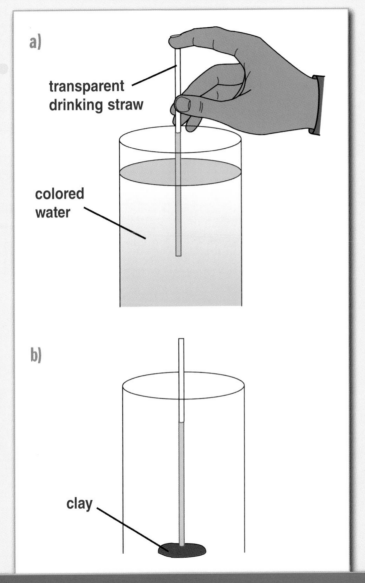

a) transparent drinking straw

colored water

b)

clay

5 a) Remove some colored water using a clear drinking straw.
  b) With your finger still on the top of the straw, push the lower end into a lump of clay. Then remove your finger. Water should not leak from the straw.

Ideas for a Science Fair Project

- Design and carry out experiments to show that water reaches its greatest density at 4°C (39°F).

- Design and do experiments to find out what happens to the density of ice as it cools to temperatures below its freezing point of 0°C (32°F).

- Show that when the distance between molecules increases ten times, the volume they occupy increases a thousand times.

Water Turnover

As winter approaches in the Northern Hemisphere, the surface water on northern lakes and ponds cools. Because the colder water is more dense than the warmer water beneath it, it sinks. The warmer water is displaced and rises to the surface. The colder water provides more oxygen to living organisms under the water because gases are more soluble in cold water than in warm water. The rising water from the lake's bottom brings nutrients up to the life-forms near the surface.

This turnover of water continues until all the water reaches 4.0°C (39.2°F). At 4.0°C, we see another of water's unique properties: it reaches its maximum density. As the surface water cools below 4.0°C, it becomes less dense and remains above the denser 4-degree water. Turnover is complete. When the surface water reaches 0°C (32°F), it begins to freeze. Continued cooling will cause warmer water under the ice to cool to 0°C and freeze, increasing the ice thickness.

If water behaved like other compounds, it would become more dense as it cooled and would form an even denser solid. Such a solid would sink rather than float. It would settle to the bottom of a lake and kill the life-forms that dwell on the bottoms of lakes and ponds.

Turnover occurs on a very large scale in oceans. In the North Atlantic, for example, cold dry winds from land chill the waters of the Gulf Stream that warm western Europe. The cold surface water becomes more dense than water beneath it, so it sinks. It then flows southward toward warmer, less dense water. It warms as it flows southward, terminating at or near the equator.

Winds then create warm currents that once again carry the water northward, forming an ongoing circulation.

These currents moderate temperatures in both northern and southern regions. For example, west winds blowing across the Gulf Stream warm western Europe. In Ireland, there is seldom a frost, while in Winnipeg, Canada, which is at a lower latitude, temperatures as low as –20°C (–4°F) are common. Similarly, the cold water that flows south prevents southern climates from being as warm as would be expected from the solar energy they receive.

Some scientists fear that global warming may change, reduce, or eliminate ocean currents. The effects could result in major changes in climate throughout the world.

2.9 Heat Capacity and Specific Heat

(An Experiment)

Things YOU will Need:

- ✓ an adult
- ✓ cooking oil
- ✓ two 7-oz foam cups
- ✓ graduated cylinder or metric measuring cup
- ✓ refrigerator
- ✓ clock or watch
- ✓ Celsius thermometer
- ✓ pen or pencil
- ✓ notebook
- ✓ immersion heater
- ✓ cold water
- ✓ electrical outlet

The ability of water to moderate Earth's temperatures depends on another of its unique characteristics—its high heat capacity. Let's examine this property of water.

The heat capacity of a sample of matter is the heat needed to raise its temperature by one degree Celsius. It takes one calorie of heat to raise the temperature of one gram (g) of water by one degree Celsius. Therefore, the heat capacity of 1 g of water is one calorie (cal) per degree Celsius (°C). The heat capacity of 100 g of water would be 100 cal/°C.

The heat capacity of one gram of a substance is called its specific heat. The specific heat of water, therefore, is 1 cal/°C.
$$\frac{1\ \text{cal/°C}}{g}$$

Hypothesis: Because cooking oil is sticky (viscous), its specific heat will be greater than 1 cal/°C.
$$\frac{1\ \text{cal/°C}}{g}$$

1. Pour 100 g of cooking oil into a foam cup. Since one milliliter of cooking oil weighs only 0.89 g, it will take 112 mL of cooking oil to weigh 100 grams.

2. Place the 112 mL of cooking oil in a refrigerator for at least one hour.

3. Add 100 grams (g) of cold water to a graduated cylinder or a metric measuring cup. Since 1 mL of water weighs 1 gram, you can simply add 100 mL of cold water into the graduated cylinder or metric measuring cup.

4. Pour the 100 g of cold water into another foam cup.

5. Measure and record the temperature and mass of the cold water.

6. Under adult supervision, put an immersion heater in the water (see Figure 6) and plug the heater into an electrical outlet for exactly 30 seconds. After 30 seconds, the adult should unplug the heater. Leave the heater in the water so that all its heat can be transferred to the water.

7. Using a thermometer, stir the water. Record the temperature when it stops rising. This is the final temperature of the water. Record the water's final temperature and its change in temperature.

8. Calculate the heat, in calories, that the immersion heater delivers in 30 seconds.

Figure 6

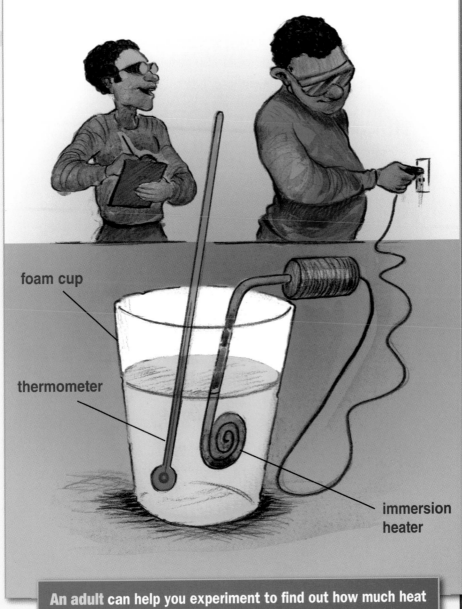

foam cup

thermometer

immersion heater

An adult can help you experiment to find out how much heat is delivered by an immersion heater in 30 seconds and to find the heat capacity of 100 grams of cooking oil.

9. Remove the cooking oil from the refrigerator. Measure and record its temperature.

10. When the heater has cooled, ask the adult to put the immersion heater in the cooking oil and plug the heater into an electrical outlet for exactly 30 seconds. The adult should unplug the heater after 30 seconds but leave it in the cooking oil.

11. Use the thermometer to stir the cooking oil. Record the cooking oil's final temperature and its change in temperature.

12. The immersion heater must have delivered the same amount of heat to the cooking oil as it did to the water. It was plugged in for the same amount of time. Therefore, how much heat, in calories, was delivered to the cooking oil?

   What was the change in temperature of the cooking oil?

   How much heat was needed to raise the temperature of 100 g of cooking oil by 1°C?

   What was the heat capacity of a 100-g sample of cooking oil. What would be the heat capacity of 200 g of cooking oil? What is the heat capacity of 1 g of cooking oil? What is the specific heat of cooking oil?

Suppose the data collected in this experiment is that shown in Table 7.

According to this data, the heat delivered by the immersion heater in 30 seconds was:

   Heat = 100 g x (30.0°C − 12.5 °C) = 1,750 cal

The heat capacity of the cooking oil was:

$$\frac{1{,}750 \text{ cal}}{34.0 \text{ °C}} = 51.5 \text{ cal/°C.}$$

The specific heat of the cooking oil was:

$$\frac{51.5 \text{ cal/°C}}{100 \text{ g}} = 0.515 \text{ cal/°C/g.}$$

How do your calculations of heat capacity and specific heat for cooking oil compare with these results?

	Water	Cooking Oil
Table 7: Data collected for determining the heat capacity and specific heat of cooking oil.		
Volume	100 mL	112 mL
Weight	100 g	100 g
Initial temp.	12.5°C	5.0°C
Final temp.	30.0°C	39.0°C
Temp. change	17.5°C	34.0°C
Heat gained	1,750 cal	1,750 cal

Ideas for a Science Fair Project

○ Under adult supervision design and do an experiment to measure the specific heat of some solids, such as aluminum, copper, lead, iron, and brass.

○ Under adult supervision, find the heat capacity and specific heat of a sample of propylene glycol (the antifreeze used in cars).

2.10 Comparing the Heat Capacities of Water and Sand

(A Demonstration)

To compare the heat capacities of different substances, you can observe how quickly equal masses of the substances warm up.

In this activity, you will put equal masses of water and sand in identical foam cups. The water can represent lakes and oceans (the heat capacities of fresh and ocean water are not very different). The sand can represent dry land. You will then cool the two substances to the same temperature.

1. Weigh two foam cups. They should be about equal in weight. Then add 100 g of water to one cup. To a second cup, add 100 g of sand.

2. Put both cups in a refrigerator. Leave them for several hours. Then check to see whether the temperatures of the contents of both cups are the same.

3. When the temperatures of the sand and water are the same, remove them from the refrigerator. Put them side by side on a kitchen counter or table. Let heat from the warm room flow into both water and sand.

Which substance warms faster? Which substance warms slower? Which substance has the greater heat capacity?

Ideas for a Science Fair Project

- Let the sand and water you used in Experiment 2.10 come to room temperature. If you put them back in a refrigerator, which substance will cool faster?
- How does water's large heat capacity account for onshore and offshore summer breezes?

Water Moderates Air Temperatures

Water's large heat capacity is the reason the temperature of large bodies of water, such as oceans and lakes changes very slowly. The air in coastal regions and areas near large lakes does not undergo the large seasonal or daily temperature changes that happen in places that are far from huge bodies of water. In deserts, where water is minimal, it may be sizzling hot during the day and freezing cold at night.

The Water Cycle

Earth's water is constantly moving. We see water in motion when raindrops fall, rivers flow, and ocean waves crash upon beaches. But there is also motion that we don't see—the motion of the tiny molecules that make up water. Water evaporates (changes from liquid to gas) from lakes, rivers, puddles, plants, and the ground. We can't see the tiny water molecules that separate when they evaporate into the air. The gaseous water becomes part of the air only to condense and fall back to Earth as rain.

Figure 7a

rain
and
snow

moist
air

rivers and ocean

The water cycle. Water evaporates into the air and returns to the ground as rain or snow.

Earth's water moves in a cycle as shown in Figure 7a. It falls from clouds as rain or snow, then evaporates and reenters the air. The quantities of water in various parts of the cycle are shown in Figure 7b.

Earth's total amount of water changes very little. It used to be thought that the volume of Earth's water is constant. But it was discovered that small comets carry snow into our atmosphere. The snow melts and vaporizes. Each comet carries about 20 to 40 tons (4,800 to 9,600 gallons) of water. Comets are believed to have added about 2,700 cubic kilometers (650 cubic miles) of water to Earth over the last 10,000 years—a tiny percentage (0.0002%) of Earth's total water.

Because water is so vital to life, we must take care to protect and conserve it. Water is being contaminated by pesticides, fertilizers, farm runoff, acid rain, and urban pollutants. There is no way to increase Earth's water so we must strive to keep what water we have.

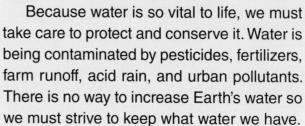

Figure 7b

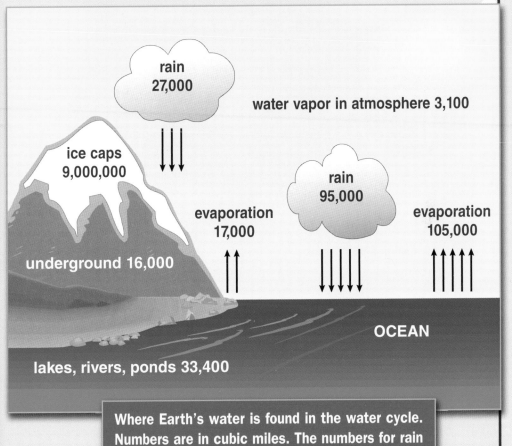

rain
27,000

water vapor in atmosphere 3,100

ice caps
9,000,000

rain
95,000

evaporation
17,000

evaporation
105,000

underground 16,000

OCEAN

lakes, rivers, ponds 33,400

Where Earth's water is found in the water cycle.
Numbers are in cubic miles. The numbers for rain
and evaporation are in cubic miles per year.

3.1 The Water Cycle: A Model

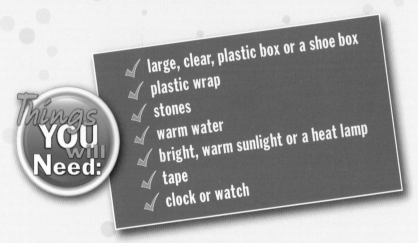

- large, clear, plastic box or a shoe box
- plastic wrap
- stones
- warm water
- bright, warm sunlight or a heat lamp
- tape
- clock or watch

1. Obtain a large, clear, plastic box, or line a shoe box with a sheet of plastic wrap.

2. Put some stones at one end of the box to represent Earth's soil and mountains.

3. Add one or two inches of warm water to the bottom of the box. The water represents Earth's oceans, lakes, and rivers, anywhere water is in contact with air.

4. Place the box in bright, warm sunlight or under a heat lamp to represent the sun. Cover the top of the box with plastic wrap. Tape the wrap to the sides of the box so that the box is sealed. (See Figure 8.)

5. Observe the box every few minutes for several hours. Can you see drops forming on the plastic cover? Where did that water come from? What must have happened to it?

   Do any of the droplets grow large enough to "rain" on the "earth" and "sea" below?

Figure 8

sunlight

water droplets plastic wrap

tape clear box water rocks

A model of Earth's water cycle can be made with water, rocks, a box, and plastic wrap.

Idea for a Science Fair Project

Design and do an experiment to measure the energy needed to change one gram of liquid water to a gas.

3.2 **How Raindrops Are Made**
(An Experiment)

Things **YOU** will **Need:**
- ✓ wide, clear plastic container that can be sealed
- ✓ 2 metal jar lids
- ✓ warm water
- ✓ table salt (sodium chloride [NaCl])

As water vapor is carried up into the atmosphere, the air expands. When air or any gas expands, it cools. With cooling, the water molecules move slower, making it possible for them to stick together. Some of the gaseous water may condense. However, atmospheric moisture may or may not form clouds, which are groups of tiny drops of water. For raindrops to form as the water cools there must be tiny particles on which the water vapor can condense. These particles are known as *condensation nuclei*. Without condensation nuclei, water vapor can cool to temperatures as low as −40°C (−40°F) without condensing.

Tiny salt crystals commonly serve as condensation nuclei. They are spattered into the air when ocean waves crash on shores. Updrafts carry the salt particles high into the air. The crystals are tiny, with diameters of about one tenth of a micron (0.0001 cm).

Hypothesis: Ordinary table salt crystals will attract water vapor, forming "raindrops."

1. Find a wide, clear plastic container that can be sealed. Put a metal jar lid, open side down, on the bottom of the container (see Figure 9).

2. Cover the bottom of the container with a shallow layer of warm water. The water should not cover the metal jar lid.

Figure 9

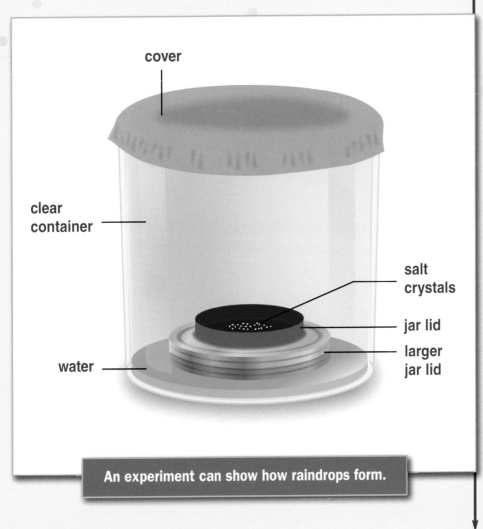

cover

clear container

salt crystals

jar lid

larger jar lid

water

An experiment can show how raindrops form.

3. Hold a second, smaller metal jar lid open side up. Add a few crystals of table salt to the second metal jar lid. Place the second jar lid on the first one.

4. Cover the plastic container to seal it. The warm water will evaporate, filling the container with water vapor.

5. Examine the salt crystals every 15 minutes. What happens to the crystals?

6. Do "raindrops" form? If drops have formed, remove the container's cover. If drops form and the air outside the container is very dry, remove the lid with the salt crystals and watch the "raindrops." Do they evaporate leaving the solid salt crystals? Was the hypothesis correct?

3.3 How Acidic Is Your Rain? (A Measurement)

- ✓ rain
- ✓ plastic container
- ✓ pH paper that can measure pH to at least ± (0.5)
- ✓ a pH unit (You may be able to borrow pH paper from your school. You can also buy it from a science supply house or a store that sells fish or swimming pool supplies.)

The atmosphere is mostly nitrogen (78 percent) and oxygen (21 percent). However, human activities have polluted the air with other gases. Growing amounts of carbon dioxide (CO_2) from the burning of fossil fuels, as well as other greenhouse gases, are causing global warming. Gases such as sulfur dioxide (SO_2) and nitrogen dioxide (NO_2) released from the smokestacks of many industries can dissolve. When these gases dissolve in atmospheric water, they form dilute sulfuric (H_2SO_4) and nitric (HNO_3) acids. When these acidic raindrops fall to earth, they may seep into the soil and make it more acidic. They also fall on limestone and marble structures, which slowly dissolve. Acid rain entering soil, lakes, ponds, and rivers may kill the eggs and seeds of various animals and plants, which affects the food webs in these environments.

Acids form hydrogen ions (H^+) in water. An acid's strength is determined by its pH, which is a measure of the concentration of hydrogen ions. Neutral substances, such as pure water, have a pH of 7.0. Acids have a pH less than 7. Substances that have a pH greater than 7 are said to be alkaline, or basic.

All rain is slightly acidic because atmospheric carbon dioxide, which makes up about 0.04 percent of atmospheric gases, is soluble in water. Dissolved carbon dioxide produces a solution that is slightly acidic, so it is quite normal to find rain with a pH as low as 5.6. Acid rain is defined as rainwater that has a pH less than 5.6.

1. To find the pH of rainwater, collect some rain in a plastic container.

2. Test the rainwater by dipping the end of a strip of pH paper into the water. You will need to use test paper that can measure pH to at least ±0.5 a pH unit. The paper should be able to distinguish pH 4.5 from pH 4.0 or pH 5.0.

3. Compare the color of the pH test paper dipped in the rainwater with a standard supplied with the test paper. The comparison will show you the rainwater's pH. What is the pH of your rainwater?

Ideas for a Science Fair Project

- Is the pH of rain at the beginning of a storm different from its pH near the end of a storm? If it is, can you explain why?
- Does the pH of rain vary from season to season? Is it, for example, more acidic in the winter than in the summer?
- Is snow acidic? How can you find out?
- Is the pH of rain affected by location? Some people say that rain in the eastern United States is more acidic than rain in the midwest or far west. How can you find out?
- What other substances such as smoke particles and engine fumes contribute to air pollution? Design ways to detect some of these substances in the air.

Effects of Acid Rain

Many lakes were normally alkaline at a pH of 8. When the pH fell to 7, concentrations of calcium in the water diminished. The eggs of some species of salamanders are so sensitive to the lower calcium concentrations that their populations are vanishing.

At a pH of 6.6, snails die; at a pH of 6, tadpoles fail to mature. If the water becomes more acidic, more life-forms die off. At a pH of 4.5, all fish die.

Acid rain falling on soil will dissolve chemical compounds containing mercury, cadmium, and lead ions, which are toxic. Microorganisms essential for decomposing organic matter succumb to these toxic substances.

Groundwater and Aquifers

When rain falls on the earth, some of it evaporates quickly or runs off into streams and rivers, which flow into ponds, lakes, or an ocean. Some is absorbed by plants. The rest seeps into the ground to groundwater. Groundwater moves slowly due to gravity, on average about 30 meters (98 ft) per year. A speed of 10 meters (33 ft) per day is considered fast. The volume of this underground water is 60 times as great as the volume of water in lakes, ponds, rivers, and clouds.

As water from rain, lakes, and rivers succumbs to gravity and sinks into the soil, it fills some of the spaces between the particles of soil and rocks. At some depth, it completely fills all these spaces; it saturates the soil with water. The level dividing the saturated soil from unsaturated soil is called the water table. The water table is the upper level of an aquifer. An aquifer is soil or rocks where large amounts of water saturate (fill the spaces between) the soil particles. In some places the water table is higher than the ground, forming a pond, lake, or swamp. You can think of an aquifer as a reservoir of water.

The depth of aquifers varies. They usually extend down to impermeable bedrock. Sometimes aquifers are layered. A layer of impermeable soil or rock will separate the upper and lower aquifers. The lower aquifer is called a confined aquifer.

Wells are drilled into aquifers so that water can be pumped from them. Groundwater pumped from wells provides water for the residents of many towns and cities. In fact, more than 50 percent of the drinking water consumed in the United States comes from the ground.

And 65 percent of the water used for irrigation is pumped from the ground. For an aquifer to provide a community with water on a continual basis, the aquifer must be recharged; that is, water must be added to the aquifer. Usually this added water is rainwater that equals or exceeds the water removed by pumping. However, some aquifers are being recharged at a slower rate than they are being pumped. As a result, the water table in these aquifers is falling. Wells have to be drilled deeper, and the cost of pumping the water becomes greater.

Aquifers can become polluted, making the water unfit to drink. There are two types of pollution. Point-source pollution comes from a single source such as a single factory, sewage plant, septic tank, gasoline station, or landfill. Non-point pollution or polluted runoff, which is the major source, includes runoff from roads, driveways, farms, lawns, and golf courses.

Finding a source of pollution is not always easy. In 1983, scientists noticed that beluga whales living around the mouth of the St. Lawrence River were dying younger than expected. Analysis of their flesh showed a high concentration of mirex, a toxic pesticide that had been banned since 1978. Mirex was not present in the river or ocean water around the whales. So how did they ingest mirex?

An investigation revealed that mirex had been been made on the shores of Lake Ontario and was still in that lake's sediment. Further study showed that the flesh of eels—a favorite food of belugas—that traveled down the St. Lawrence from Lake Ontario were rich in mirex. The mystery was solved. The eels were transporting mirex from Lake Ontario to the whales that ate them in the Gulf of St. Lawrence.

The Ogallala

The Ogallala Aquifer, which was formed by melting glaciers several million years ago, is huge. It lies under most of Nebraska as well as parts of South Dakota, Wyoming, Colorado, Kansas, Oklahoma, New Mexico, and Texas. Farmers in these states pump water from the Ogallala to irrigate their crops of corn, cotton, and sorghum and to provide water for their cattle.

The recharge rate of this aquifer is very low—about one-tenth the rate at which it is being pumped. As a result, this aquifer will soon be dry. Until then, the cost of its water is increasing because it has to be pumped from greater depths every year. Some farmers have been forced out of business. Others are switching to crops that require less water.

Similar problems with aquifers exist throughout the world. And a rising world population only compounds the problem.

Fighting Urban Runoff Pollution

The Environmental Protection Agency (EPA) has shown that when rain falls faster than it can be absorbed, urban runoff is a major source of water pollution. The runoff waters emptying into storm drains carry oil, road salts, pesticides, bacteria, and heavy metals. These pollutants reach rivers, wetlands, lakes, and oceans. The problem can be reduced by planting rain gardens. These gardens are depressions 15 to 30 cm (6 to 12 in) deep where native plants grow. The gardens can capture much of the runoff water and filter pollutants as the water seeps into the soil and underlying aquifers.

Eels that traveled in the St. Lawrence River were contaminated with the toxic pesticide mirex. Beluga whales that ate the eels died younger than expected.

Such gardens should be sited in the path of runoff waters from rain, down spouts, gutters, driveways, sidewalks, or at the base of sloped ground. They should not be near a building's foundation, buried utility pipes and wires, or septic drainage fields.

At the base of a rain garden, there is typically a drainpipe, such as perforated PVC, slanted toward a storm drain. The pipe is covered with a layer of gravel covered by soil—compost, sand, and topsoil in a 2:5:3 ratio. Native plants can be added to this upper layer. Their roots will hold the soil, and they will need minimal care. A layer of mulch prevents weeds and removes metals from the runoff.

3.4 A Model Aquifer

Things YOU will Need:

✓ aquarium, clear plastic shoe box, or large bowl
✓ sand
✓ ruler
✓ water
✓ food coloring
✓ clay
✓ watering can

You can make a model aquifer.

1. Cover the bottom of an aquarium, clear plastic shoe box, or large clear bowl with a layer of clay. The glass or plastic can represent an impermeable layer of bedrock under the soil.

2. Add a layer of sand about 7 to 10 cm (3 to 4 in) deep. Use the sand to form model hills and valleys. The lowest "valley" in the sand should have a depth of at least a centimeter (1/2 in) above the "bedrock."

3. Sprinkle colored water from a watering can onto the sand. From the side, watch the "rain" sink into the soil.

4. Observe the formation of a water table.

5. Add more "rain" and watch the water table rise. Notice how "ponds" are created as the water table rises.

6. Create a "drought." Add no more water for several days. Watch ponds dry up as the water table falls. Then add more "rain" and notice the rising level of the aquifer's water table.

Idea for a Science Fair Project

What might cause water to move in an aquifer? Develop a hypothesis and an experiment to test a conclusion of your hypothesis.

Nitrogen, Phosphorus, and Wastewater Problems

The tiny plants at the base of the food web in saltwater estuaries need nitrogen and phosphorus compounds. However, if there is too much of these chemicals, algae will grow rapidly. The water becomes green and murky. When this excess plant life dies, the microbes that decompose it carry on respiration which removes oxygen from the water. Without enough oxygen, fish and other marine life die. The algae also block the sunlight from reaching deeper plants. This prevents valuable marine plants, such as eelgrass, from carrying on photosynthesis, so they die as well.

The sources of polluting nitrogen are wastewater, which contains urine; fertilizers from farms, golf courses, and lawns; acid rain; and rain or melted snow runoff that carries feces, dirt, and trash. These nitrogen sources dissolve in groundwater and filter down to an aquifer that seeps into nearby estuaries.

The chemicals that foster algal growth and thus limit plant and animal growth in freshwater are chemical compounds containing phosphorus. The phosphorus comes from a variety of sources—acid rain, wastewater, fertilizers, runoff, and soil erosion. Although phosphate compounds, which contain phosphorus, have been removed from laundry detergents, they are still present in many automatic dishwasher detergents. Some states are requiring that these detergents, a common source of phosphorus in freshwater, contain no more than trace amounts of phosphates.

In most communities that do not have public sewer systems, homes flush human waste into septic tanks. Each septic tank is connected to a leach field, where liquid wastes flow from the tank and filter through the ground. After percolating through soil below the leach field, most of the bacteria and viruses are removed. However, some of the nutrients, such as nitrogen and phosphorus, may enter the groundwater and eventually reach lakes, ponds, rivers, or oceans.

Septic tanks trap and store solid waste. Bacteria decompose the organic matter. Inorganic and some solid organic matter sink to the tank's bottom as a sludge.

Septic tanks are pumped periodically to remove the solid waste. Pumper trucks transport the waste to facilities that treat the waste in a manner similar to the way it is treated in a municipal wastewater system.

Some towns and cities treat wastewater so thoroughly that it can be returned safely to the water supply or into the ground, where it filters into an aquifer. Soil bacteria act on the wastewater from septic tanks, removing harmful viruses and breaking it down into substances that are safe to drink. However, if a well is too close to a septic tank, the wastewater may contaminate the well water. Bacteria convert the nitrogen in urine to nitrates (compounds that contain the nitrate ion NO_3^-) before it is changed to the element nitrogen (N_2). A high concentration of nitrates in well water serves as an indicator. It shows that the waste-water has not been filtered well. It may be necessary to drill a new well farther from the septic tank's leach field.

3.5 Pumping and Polluting an Aquifer (A Model)

Things YOU will Need:

- ✓ dry sand
- ✓ large, clear plastic vial (30–50 mL)
- ✓ eyedropper
- ✓ water
- ✓ green food coloring

1. To make an aquifer, add dry sand to a large, clear plastic vial until it is about about three-quarters full.

2. Use an eyedropper to make "rain" fall on the sand. Watch the water trickle down through the sand. Continue "raining" until a "pond" covers the aquifer.

3. To make a "well" in the aquifer, push an eyedropper to the bottom of the vial at one side of your aquifer (see Figure 10).

4. Use the eyedropper as a "pump" to remove water from the aquifer. Pump out as much water as possible. What happens to an aquifer's water table if is pumped faster than it is recharged?

5. Next, "pollute" the aquifer by adding one drop of green food coloring to the sand.

6. "Rain" clear water onto the sand again. What happens to the "pollution?"

Figure 10

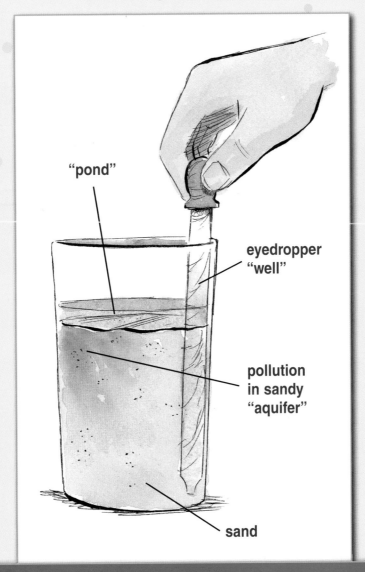

"pond"

eyedropper
"well"

pollution
in sandy
"aquifer"

sand

Use an eyedropper to make a "well" in a sandy "aquifer." The eyedropper can also be used to pump water from the "aquifer."

7. Pump the aquifer again. Rain on and then pump the aquifer several times. Does the well become polluted?

8. Do an experiment to see if the pollution can be removed by many rains and pumpings.

How might a polluted aquifer be cleaned up?

Ideas for a Science Fair Project

- Make a hypothesis to explain how water gets from the ground to your water faucets. Then test your hypothesis.
- Make a hypothesis to explain what happens to your home's wastewater. Then test your hypothesis.

3.6 Why Seawater and Freshwater Tend Not to Mix

(A Demonstration)

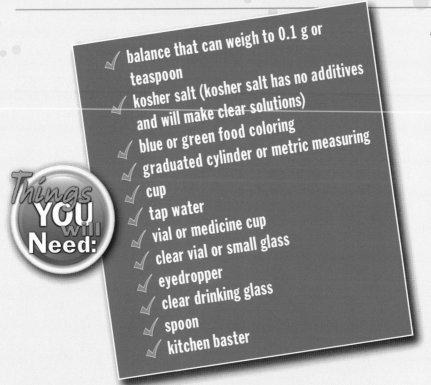

Things YOU will Need:

- ✓ balance that can weigh to 0.1 g or teaspoon
- ✓ kosher salt (kosher salt has no additives and will make clear solutions)
- ✓ blue or green food coloring
- ✓ graduated cylinder or metric measuring cup
- ✓ tap water
- ✓ vial or medicine cup
- ✓ clear vial or small glass
- ✓ eyedropper
- ✓ clear drinking glass
- ✓ spoon
- ✓ kitchen baster

Aquifers near the ocean often become polluted by salt water. Normally, the top of an aquifer is above sea level. Pressure from the depth of the freshwater and density differences keep the salt water from intruding into the freshwater. During a drought or excessive pumping of the aquifer, the water table may fall below sea level. Seawater will then mix with the freshwater. If the mixing is extensive, the water may no longer be fit to drink. To see how differences in density tend to keep keep fresh-water and salt water apart, you can do the following steps.

1. To make some seawater, add 3.4 grams (one teaspoon) of kosher salt to 100 mL of cold tap water. Stir until all the salt dissolves.

2. Pour some of the salt water into a vial or medicine cup. Add several drops of food coloring. Stir until the color is uniform.

3. Pour some cold tap water into a clear vial or small glass.

4. Use an eyedropper to remove some of the colored salt water.

5. Put the tip of the eyedropper into the clear cold water. Slowly squeeze the bulb of the eyedropper (Figure 11a). What happens to the salt water? Does it go up or down in the tap water? What does this tell you about the density of salt water?

6. Use an eyedropper to add a drop of colored cold water to a vial of clear salt water. What do you predict will happen? Try it. Was your prediction correct?

7. Prepare a saturated solution of salt. Add a spoonful of kosher salt to a glass that is about one-third full of warm water. Stir with a spoon. Continue to add salt and stir until no more salt will dissolve. A small amount of salt will remain on the bottom of the glass.

8. Add a few drops of blue or green food coloring to the saturated salt solution and stir.

9. Add cold water to a clear glass or plastic cup until it is half full.

10. Squeeze the bulb of a kitchen baster. Then put the baster's nozzle at the bottom of the colored salt solution. *Slowly* release the bulb, drawing the colored liquid into the baster.

Figure 11a

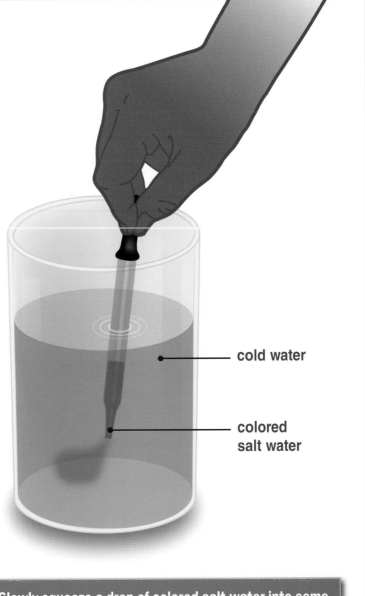

cold water

colored
salt water

Slowly squeeze a drop of colored salt water into some clear, cold water. What happens to the salt water? Does it sink or float?

11. Remove the baster from the glass. Carefully lower the baster's nozzle to the bottom of the glass of cold water. *Very slowly* squeeze the bulb to form a colored layer of salt water under the clear water (Figure 11b.) *Keep the bulb squeezed* as you slowly remove the baster from the water. You should now have a distinct colored layer under the clear water.

12. Carefully move the glass containing the two liquid layers to a quiet place where it will not be disturbed.

13. Observe the layers each day. What do you notice? What evidence do you have that molecules of salt are slowly diffusing into the clear water?

Figure 11b

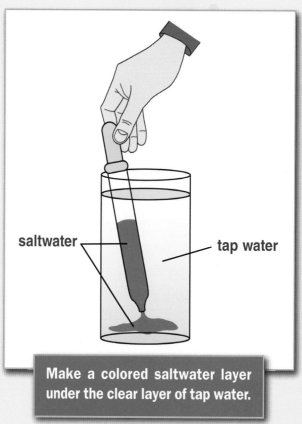

saltwater tap water

Make a colored saltwater layer under the clear layer of tap water.

3.7 How Much Space Is There Between Soil Particles?

(A Measurement)

Things YOU will Need:

- ✓ dry sand
- ✓ graduated cylinder
- ✓ notebook
- ✓ pen or pencil
- ✓ plastic or foam cup
- ✓ water

In an aquifer, water fills the spaces between the particles of soil and rock. In this activity you will try to find what percentage of the space in a sandy aquifer is occupied by water.

1. Pour dry sand into a graduated cylinder until it is about two-thirds full. Record the volume of sand.

2. Then pour the sand into a plastic or foam cup.

3. Add water to the graduated cylinder until it is about one-third full. Record the volume of the water.

4. Carefully pour the sand from the cup into the water in the graduated cylinder. The water will fill the spaces between the grains of sand. What is the volume of the sand and water together?

5. What percentage of the sandy aquifer is actually water? What percentage is sand?

Suppose the volume of dry sand with air was 70 cm³ (70 mL). When the dry sand was added to 35 cm³ of water, the total volume became 75 cm³. There must have been a measureable amount of air between the dry sand particles. The volume of the dry sand grains alone must have been:

volume of sand and water together − volume of water = volume of sand

$$75 \text{ cm}^3 - 35 \text{ cm}^3 = 40 \text{ cm}^3$$

volume of dry sand with air − volume of sand without air = volume of air in the sand

$$70 \text{ cm}^3 - 40 \text{ cm}^3 = 30 \text{ cm}^3$$

Now those spaces are filled with water; therefore, the percentage of the space occupied by water is

$$\frac{30 \text{ cm}^3}{70 \text{ cm}^3} = 0.43 = 43\%$$

Ideas for a Science Fair Project

○ What percentage of a gravel-filled aquifer would be water?

○ Does the shape of the particles affect the amount of space between the particles? Design and do experiments to find out.

3.8 **Transpiration**
(A Demonstration)

Things YOU will Need:

- ✓ small jar
- ✓ water
- ✓ scissors
- ✓ cardboard
- ✓ clear plastic cup
- ✓ nail
- ✓ petroleum jelly
- ✓ small healthy leaf such as a maple leaf
- ✓ sunny place
- ✓ stone

Land plants obtain their water from the ground. Water between the soil particles is absorbed by the roots and moves up the plant by capillary action. As you read in Chapter 2, the evaporation of water from a plant creates a tension that, together with capillarity and water's cohesiveness, draws water up the narrow tubes within even the tallest trees.

The evaporation of water from the leaves of plants is called transpiration. On the underside of leaves are tiny openings called stomata. (See Figure 12a.) Water evaporates from plant leaves through these stomata. Guard cells are found on either side of each stoma. The guard cells come together and close the stoma during dry weather. They swell and open the stoma when water is plentiful. You can witness transpiration by doing the following steps.

Figure 12a

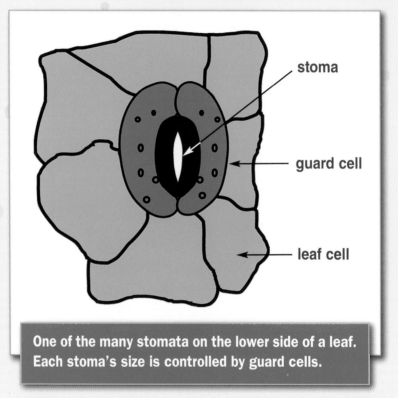

stoma

guard cell

leaf cell

One of the many stomata on the lower side of a leaf. Each stoma's size is controlled by guard cells.

1. Nearly fill a small jar with water.

2. Cut a square piece of cardboard that will more than cover the mouth of the jar.

3. Use a nail to make a small hole in the center of the cardboard.

4. Carefully remove a small, healthy leaf from a shade tree such as a maple. Be sure to include all of the leaf's stem (petiole). Put the petiole through the hole in the cardboard. Then put the cardboard on the mouth of the jar so that the lower end of the leaf's petiole is in the water, as shown in Figure 12b.

Figure 12b

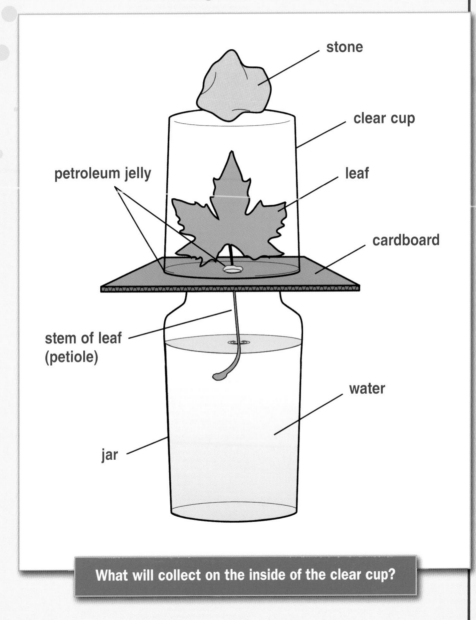

stone

clear cup

petroleum jelly

leaf

cardboard

stem of leaf
(petiole)

water

jar

What will collect on the inside of the clear cup?

5. Spread a layer of petroleum jelly around the rim of a clear plastic cup. Also use the petroleum jelly to seal the space around the petiole where it passes through the cardboard.

6. Invert the cup over the leaf. The petroleum jelly will prevent gases from entering or leaving the cup through its mouth or through the hole in the cardboard.

7. Put the device in a sunny place. If there is a breeze and you place it outside, put a stone on the plastic cup to prevent it from moving.

8. After an hour or two, look at the cup. What do you see collecting on the inside of the inverted cup? What do you think it is? How could it have gotten there?

Idea for a Science Fair Project

Prepare a microscope slide of tissue from the lower side of a geranium leaf. Examine the tissue under a microscope. You will see stomata and guard cells. Determine the number of stomata per square centimeter. Use that information to calculate the number of stomata on an average leaf. Then estimate the number of stomata on the plant.

Rivers, Lakes, Dams, Reservoirs, and Wetlands

The groundwater and runoff water that drain from a land area into a river or lake is called a watershed. A watershed usually generates a number of small streams that join to form a river. The watershed of the Mississippi River covers 32 million square kilometers (12 million square miles). Lakes are the source of some rivers. The St. Lawrence River, for example, flows out of Lake Ontario.

Before trains and automobiles existed, rivers were used as a main means of transportation. Today, they are still highways for boats, but they also are used to produce electrical power, provide drinking water, and carry away wastewater.

Rivers carry soil from their banks and from the land they flow through. Much of that soil is deposited as

Crater Lake in Oregon

sediment at the river's mouth. A million tons of sediment is deposited at the mouth of the Mississippi each year. That seems like a lot of dirt, but five times as much is deposited at the mouth of the Amazon River in Brazil.

Lakes have formed in several ways. Some, such as the lakes in East Africa, formed after movement of Earth's crust formed rift valleys, and water accumulated in those valleys. Others, such as Oregon's Crater Lake, fill the craters of inactive volcanoes. Still others were created when water filled the huge hollows left by glaciers. The Great Lakes of North America, which hold 18 percent of the world's surface freshwater, were created in this way. Glaciers also created kettle ponds. Retreating glaciers left blocks of ice buried in sediments. When the ice melted, kettle ponds were formed.

Water enters lakes from rivers and streams, groundwater, rain, and runoff. Some water leaves lakes in rivers or because it is withdrawn by a public water supply. All lakes lose water by evaporation and seepage into the ground.

Rivers, lakes, ponds, reservoirs, and aquifers contain the freshwater we drink. To keep this water "green" we must guard it from contamination.

4.1 A Stream's Water Flow (A Measurement)

It is important to know how much water is flowing in a river. At a certain rate of flow, a river will flood. Melting snow or heavy rains may cause a river to swell and overflow its banks, creating floods that can cause great damage. By measuring the volume of water flowing in a river per unit time, flooding downstream can be predicted, and cities and towns can prepare or be evacuated.

This experiment, which should be done **under adult supervision**, will help you to see how a river's rate of flow can be measured.

1. Find a relatively shallow stream, one that you can safely wade. At some point along the stream, use a tape measure to find its width. Record that width in your notebook.

2. Place markers (stakes will do) at equal distances (5 meters is a good choice) up- and downstream from the point where you measured the stream's width.

3. Drop an orange into the stream at different distances from the bank. The orange will float past the two markers that you placed along one shore (see Figure 13a). Use the orange, the stakes, and a stopwatch to measure the stream's velocity at different distances from the riverbank. Start the watch when the orange passes the upstream stake. Stop the watch when the orange crosses the downstream stake. Try to make four or five measurements at equally spaced positions across the stream.

Suppose at one position it takes the orange 10.0 seconds (s) to travel the distance between markers that are 10 meters apart. The stream's velocity at that point in the stream would be

$$10.0 \text{ m}/ 10.0 \text{ s} = 1.0 \text{ m/s}$$

Record the velocity at several distances from the riverbank. Where does the stream flow fastest? Slowest? Calculate the average speed of the stream.

4. At the crossing where you measured the stream's width, determine the stream's depth at 4 or 5 equally spaced positions across the stream. Again, calculate the stream's average depth.

5. From your measurements, calculate the volume of water moving downriver per second.

For example, let's assume the stream's width was 5.0 meters, the average velocity was 1.0 m/s, and the average depth was 0.3 m. The river's cross-section can be considered to be a rectangle with a width of 5.0 m and a depth of 0.3 m. Its area, therefore, would be:

$$5.0 \text{ m} \times 0.3 \text{ m} = 1.5 \text{ m}^2.$$

Figure 13

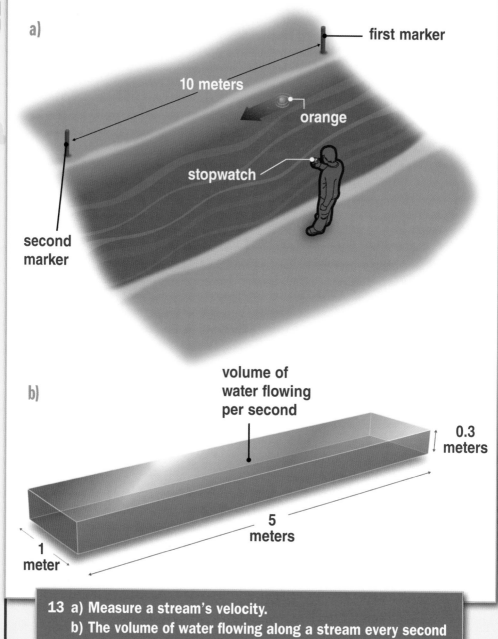

a)

first marker

10 meters

orange

stopwatch

second
marker

b)

volume of
water flowing
per second

0.3
meters

5
meters

1
meter

13 a) Measure a stream's velocity.
   b) The volume of water flowing along a stream every second

Since the average velocity is 1.0 m/s, a volume of water equal to 1.5 m³ flows past any point along the stream every second (see Figure 13b).

$$1.5 \text{ m}^2 \times 1.0 \text{ m/s} = 1.5 \text{ m}^3/\text{s} \ (1{,}500 \text{ L/s or } 397 \text{ gal/s})$$

For most major rivers that flood, engineers calculate normal river flow. They use that information and measurements of river depths at several points upriver from areas that flood to predict a river's flood stage.

Idea for a Science Fair Project

Measure a stream's flow volume at different times of the year. When is the flow volume greatest? When is it least? Try to explain your results.

Floods and Dams

As you read in Chapter 2, floods are sometimes beneficial. They can bring new soil and replenish nutrients removed by farming. More commonly, however, they cause damage, disease, and death.

In Colonial America, land was plentiful, so people wisely built their homes on high land above any threat of flooding. But fertile plains that had been nourished by earlier floods attracted farmers. During the industrial revolution, factories, which needed water to manufacture their goods and ships to transport the goods, were built along riverbanks. Homes to house factory workers multiplied and cities grew. Even after destructive floods, industries and people returned to be near the rivers.

Look at a map of the United States or the world. Notice how many major cities are near a river, lake, or ocean.

Around the world, two-thirds of the riverwater headed for the oceans is obstructed by dams. Dams have been built on many rivers to control flooding as well as to generate electricity. Within a short time after a dam is built, a lake forms behind the dam. The lake can serve as a water source for nearby cities and towns, provide water to irrigate farmland, and provide boating and other water recreation for people. Of the 845,000 dams across the globe, 80,000 are in the United States. The total volume of water behind U.S. dams is 1,355 cubic kilometers (325 cubic miles). Hoover Dam is America's largest. Lake Mead, which was formed by this dam, contains 34 million cubic meters (1.2 billion cubic feet) of water.

However, dams can create problems. They flood the land behind them, forcing people out of their homes and changing the ecology of entire areas. Floodwaters can build up behind a dam, increasing the pressure on the dam's walls. In June 1976, one-third of the Teton Dam in Idaho collapsed, releasing a 20-foot high bank of water into the Snake River Valley.

As water behind a new dam floods an area, animals that breathe air drown or are forced to other terrain, and land plants are killed. As these plants decay, bacteria change naturally occurring mercury to methyl mercury, a more toxic chemical. Fish eating the plants and bacteria tend to store the mercury compound in their fat cells. As a result, the concentration of mercury in the fish becomes much greater than in the water. Even though the water may be safe to drink, the fish may not be safe to eat. Those who do eat the fish risk mercury poisoning, which can cause brain damage or death.

The oxygen content of deep water behind dams is often so low that when it is released, it cannot support life downstream. Below a dam, fish such as salmon cannot return to their upstream spawning grounds unless fish ladders are constructed beside the dam.

As water builds up behind a dam, the flow of water in the river or rivers leading to the dam is slowed. This causes sediments to build up, which clogs riverbeds and fills the lake behind the dam.

Wetlands

Wetlands—marshes, swamps, bogs, and fens—are vital biomes. They are home to vast numbers of animals and plants that cannot survive elsewhere. They reduce flooding because their spongelike nature can absorb large volumes of water. They purify water. They can take in large quantities of pollutants, such as sewage and farm and feedlot runoff. The wetland plants remove these chemicals from the water before the water reaches streams and rivers.

Marshes are filled with low-growing plants, such as cattails and pickerel weed, yet they still have considerable open water. Swamps are home to shrubs and trees that can survive flooding. Bogs and fens develop in colder parts of the world. The low temperatures reduce bacterial action and, therefore, the rate of decomposition of dead plants. As this plant matter accumulates, it forms peat. The northern part of North America contains more than one-third of the world's peat bogs. These bogs hold few nutrients and are very

This earthen dam created a reservoir of freshwater.

acidic. Only some plants, such as sphagnum moss, heather, pitcher plants, and black spruce, can grow there.

Urbanization and Wetlands

By 2010, half of the wetlands, which once constituted 10 percent of the continental United States, had been destroyed. Developers and farmers regarded wetlands as building sites or potential farmland that could be filled for their purposes, and they often were.

Building towns and cities on former wetlands has had unfortunate effects. Removing the spongy soil that absorbs water and pollutants increases the danger of floods. In its place are concrete and asphalt from which water simply runs off into storm drains, carrying with it a host of pollutants—litter, wastewater, oil and gasoline from streets, pesticides and fertilizers from lawns, small-animal feces, and other toxic substances.

Some cities try to combat the problem by planting trees and other vegetation along streets, around parking lots, and in parks. The plants absorb soil water and reduce the pollutants that might flow into public water sources. Roof gardens ("green roofs") can provide fresh vegetables, and cisterns can collect rainwater. The collected rainwater reduces runoff and urban pollution while providing water to irrigate the plants.

4.2 Aquatic Wetland Plants and Animals
(An Experiment)

Do this experiment under adult supervision. If you have not used a binocular microscope or prepared microscope slides, work with someone who has.

Hypothesis: Water from a wetland or pond will contain a variety of plants and small animals.

1. Gather some water from a wetland. If a wetland is not available, use water from a pond.

2. Using an eyedropper, place a drop of the wetland water on a microscope slide.

3. Examine the drop under the microscope. What kind of plants and animals do you see? Some may be moving too fast for you to observe them. You may be able to trap them by adding some fluffy cotton to the water and adding a coverslip.

   Do you see any plants or animals like the ones shown in Figure 14?

Figure 14

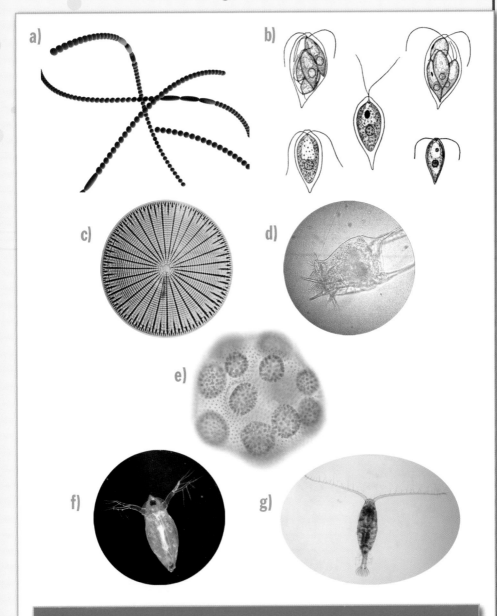

14 **Some living things you might find in wetlands or pond water:**
a) green bacteria; b) green one-cell plants; c) diatoms; d) rotifers;
e) colony of green one-cell plants; f) water fleas; g) copepod.

4. Plant cells that are green probably contain chlorophyll. Such plants are able to carry on photosynthesis and manufacture food from carbon dioxide, water, and solar energy.

Was the hypothesis correct?

Conserving Water, a Precious Resource

Approximately 5.8 billion liters (1.5 billion gallons) of water flow each day from the Catskill Mountains to the city of New York. Giant tunnels carry the water to the city, where it is distributed through more than 6,000 miles of pipe. The population of New York City is approximately 8 million people. Do the division and you see that water consumption per person per day in New York is about 725 liters (190 gallons). Of course, not all that water is used by people. Businesses, industries, and power plants use a good part of it.

As you read in Chapter 1, domestic use of water in the United States accounts for only 10 percent of the

water used each day. Industries and power plants are finding ways to recycle water and reduce their usage. In this chapter you will learn how you can conserve water in your home and school, thereby reducing domestic use of this precious resource.

5.1 Conserve Water, Don't Let It Leak Away (A Measurement)

Water often leaks away without ever being used. Such leaks waste a lot of water.

1. To see why, open a faucet so that about one drop comes out every second. Place a large measuring cup under the faucet. Let the drips continue to fall into the cup for several hours.

2. How much water collected in the cup over several hours? How much water would be wasted in a day? In a week? A month? A year?

Idea for a Science Fair Project

Check with your town or city's water commissioner. Do the pipes in the city's water mains have leaks? How much water leaks away each year? Given what the city charges for water, how much is the lost water worth? Why haven't any leaks been fixed?

5.2 Is the Water in Your Home Leaking Away?
(An Experiment)

Things YOU will Need:
- ✓ water meter or water pressure gauge on pump or water tank
- ✓ pen or pencil
- ✓ notebook
- ✓ clock

Hypothesis: Water is leaking from your home. This experiment checks on the hypothesis.

1. Ask permission to stay up after everyone has gone to bed. If you have a water meter, record the meter reading. If you don't have a meter, go to step 3.

2. Several hours later, read the meter again. Has the reading changed? If it has and no one has used any water, there is a leak somewhere. If not, your home is free of leaks.

3. If your home does not have a water meter, it probably has its own water that is pumped from a well. Check with a parent to be sure this is the case. Shallow wells have a pump in the basement. Deep wells have a pump in the well.

4. Ask permission to stay up after everyone has gone to bed. Look at the pressure gauge on the pump or water tank. Record the pressure. Be sure no more water is used.

5. Several hours later, read the pressure gauge again. If the pressure has dropped and no one has used any water, water is leaking somewhere. If not, your home is free of leaks.

Was the hypothesis correct?

5.3 Conserve Water: Find the Leaks in Your Home
(Measurements)

Things YOU will Need:
- ✓ container
- ✓ clock
- ✓ measuring cup
- ✓ pocket calculator (optional)
- ✓ green or blue food coloring

If you have reason to believe there are water leaks in your home, you can try to find them.

1. Watch each faucet and shower head for a several minutes. If drops fall out and you are sure the device is turned off, you know it is leaking.

2. Find out how badly it is leaking. Put a container under the leaking faucet and record the time.

3. Return several hours later. Record the new time. Pour the water that leaked into a measuring cup. What volume of water leaked?

4. Calculate the volume of water leaking per hour, per day, per month, and per year.

Show your results to your parents and suggest that the leak or leaks be fixed.

5. Leaking toilets can waste a lot of water. To see if a toilet is leaking, add green or blue food coloring to the water in the tank. After a few minutes, look at the water in the toilet bowl. Is the water in the bowl slightly blue or green? If it is, the toilet is leaking.

Let a parent know about the leak. A small adjustment may be all that is needed to fix it.

Idea for a Science Fair Project

How much water is used each time a toilet in your home is flushed? Find a way to measure the water used per flush. Keep track of the number of times the toilet is flushed. Then calculate the water used per day to flush the toilet. How much water is used per year to flush the toilets in your home?

5.4 Bath or Shower?
(An Experiment)

Things YOU will Need:
- ✓ 2 plastic pails
- ✓ pen or pencil
- ✓ notebook
- ✓ bathtub
- ✓ shower head
- ✓ clock or watch that can measure seconds

Hypothesis: If you spend as much time in the shower as you do while taking a bath, a shower will use more water.

To check up on the hypothesis, you can do experiments.

1. You can measure the volume of water you use when you take a bath. Find out what volume of water is needed to fill each of two plastic pails. Record the volume of water held by each pail.

2. Take the pails into the bathroom when you plan to take a bath.

3. Close the bathtub drain. Let water flow into one pail. When it is full, place the second pail under the faucet and pour the water in the first bucket into the tub.

4. Continue filling and emptying pails of water until the tub is filled to your liking. Record the number of pails of water you used to prepare your bath. Later, you can calculate the volume of water you used to take a bath.

5. To measure the water used to take a shower, use the same pails to collect water flowing from the shower head. Collect water from the shower head for one minute. How much water flowed from the shower head in one minute? How much water would be used if someone took a five-minute shower? A two-minute shower?

For example, suppose you find that 4 gallons of water flows from the shower head in one minute. Then a five-minute shower would use:

$$5 \text{ min} \times 4 \text{ gal/min} = 20 \text{ gal}$$

In your bathroom, how does the water used to take a five-minute shower compare with the water used to take a bath?

6. Let your family know the results of your experiment. Should you recommend that they take baths or showers? What time limit would you recommend for showers?

Was the hypothesis correct?

Ideas for a Science Fair Project

- Compare the water used per minute for a low-flow showerhead and a regular showerhead. Would it be economical to replace regular shower heads with low-flow heads?

- Take a shower in which you get wet, turn off the water while you soap up, and then rinse off. Compare the water needed to take such a shower with one in which you let the water flow throughout the shower.

Ways to Conserve Water

In the Bathroom

- Install low-flow faucets and showerheads.

- Replace old toilets with low-flush toilets that use only 6 liters (1.6 gallons) per flush. Or put sealed stone- or sand-filled bottles in toilet tanks to take up space normally occupied by water. Be sure enough water remains to adequately flush the toilet.

- Report or repair leaky faucets and toilets.

- Flush toilets only when necessary. Never use toilets as trash cans.

- Take short showers instead of baths.

- Don't let water run while brushing your teeth or soaping your hands or face.

- Never use a toilet to flush away toxic or hazardous waste materials. They can seep into and contaminate drinking water.

In the Kitchen, Laundry, and Basement

- Use a dishwasher only when it is full. Use the minimum number of washes or rinses and let dishes air dry. Use detergents that do not contain phosphates.

- Do not run water continuously when washing dishes in the sink.

- When replacing a washing machine, consider buying a front-loading machine. They use less water and energy.

- Do not use a garbage disposal in your sink. It requires lots of water and can add grease and solids to a sewage or septic system.

- Do not pour hazardous wastes down your drains or add to trash. Most towns and cities have special days when hazardous wastes are collected.

- Avoid using laundry detergents with brighteners. Brightening compounds can kill fish and other aquatic life. They also biodegrade slowly.

Outdoors and in the Garage

- Control erosion due to water by planting trees and shrubs.

- If you have a lawn, cut grass no shorter than three inches. This will promote healthy turf, which holds rainwater, filters sediments and chemicals, and requires less watering.

- Do not use fertilizers or insecticides on your lawn. They pollute groundwater.

- Water lawns and gardens only when necessary. Water early in the morning or after sunset. Otherwise, much of the water evaporates.

- Use a broom—not a hose—to clean driveways and walks.

- Wash your car only when necessary. Use a bucket and hose with a shutoff nozzle.

Avoid Pollution, Make You Own Cleaners**

- Prepare a handy all-purpose cleaner by mixing 1/4 cup of white vinegar, 2 teaspoons of borax, and 2 teaspoons of lemon juice in a one-quart spray bottle. Fill with hot water and shake. As an alternative, keep two spray bottles handy, one with white vinegar, a second with 3% hydrogen peroxide. (Be sure to store in separate spray bottles; the two react chemically if kept in the same bottle.) Spray with both liquids, then rinse with water.

- In place of bleach, use the sun to whiten white clothes.

- To make a carpet cleaner, add club soda or a 1:1 mixture of white vinegar and water. Blot dry with a cloth or paper towel.

** You may find commercial cleaners with similar ingredients. Work with an adult when making cleaners.

- Prepare a floor cleaner by adding equal amounts (1/4 cup) of baking soda and borax to a mop pail of warm water. For vinyl floors, add 1 cup of white vinegar to one gallon of warm water.

- A glass (window) cleaner can be made by mixing 2 tablespoon of white vinegar, 1 teaspoon of lemon juice, and 1 teaspoon of liquid soap in 1 quart of warm water. Keep in a spray bottle for ready use.

- A scouring cleanser paste can be made from baking soda and white vinegar.

- To clean a toilet bowl, add 1/4 cup of baking soda and 1/2 cup of white vinegar to the toilet bowl. Let stand a few minutes. Then brush well before flushing.

- To clean a paintbrush: For oil-based paints, use a commercial citrus-based solvent. For latex paints, use soap and water.

- To deodorize your refrigerator, add an open box of baking soda. For carpets or upholstery, sprinkle on baking soda, wait a few minutes, then vacuum.

- To remove mildew, add equal amounts (1/2 cup) of white vinegar and borax to 1 quart of hot water. Add the solution to a spray bottle. Spray the solution on the mildew and leave for about ten minutes. Wipe clean with dry cloths.

- Make a wood polish by adding 1 tablespoon of lemon oil to one pint of olive oil. Rub wood with cloth dipped in the liquid polish. Buff with a soft cloth.

- To clean painted walls, woodwork, and Venetian blinds add 1 cup of household ammonia, 1/2 cup of white vinegar, and 1/4 cup of baking soda to 1 gallon of warm water. Wipe the solution over surfaces with a sponge and rinse with clear water.

- Clean and deodorize a microwave oven by heating 1/4 cup of white vinegar and 1 cup of water in the microwave.

- Remove corrosion from a shower head or a faucet by soaking them in white vinegar overnight, or saturate a towel with vinegar and wrap it around the showerhead or faucet.

- Remove bathtub films, wipe with white vinegar, then with baking soda. Rinse with water.

Protect Your Family and the Water in Your Environment

- Don't buy bottled water. The Union of Concerned Scientists reports that the purity checks on tap water are better than those on bottled water. In addition, the plastic bottles the water comes in are seldom recycled and the plastic is not biodegradable. Find a reusable bottle to carry water or other liquids to school or sundry places.

- Soaps and detergents are biodegradable. They can be washed down sink and tub drains. However, most other commercial cleaners should not be washed away. Oven and toilet bowl cleaners, bleach, and drain openers are poisonous.

- Read labels. If you see words, such as *danger, warning, toxic, corrosive, flammable, poison, lye,* or *phenols,* then the products are probably hazardous. Keep such materials out of the reach of children. Never remove their labels or transfer them to other containers. And never mix them with other substances. They could react chemically and ignite or explode. If containers are corroded, ask your fire department how the containers can be moved to a hazardous waste collection site.

- Oil-based paints and solvents should be taken to a hazardous waste collection site. For latex paint, remove the lid and let the water evaporate. The can and remaining solid can be put in normal trash cans.

- Avoid using herbicides and pesticides. They can pollute the aquifer and other water sources.

119

Computers, televisions, cell phones, fluorescent and compact fluorescent lightbulbs, smoke detectors, and some thermometers contain mercury and possibly other heavy metals, such as cadmium, lead, and arsenic. Such materials should be taken to a recycling center. Most landfills and transfer stations provide services for disposal of heavy metals. Alkaline batteries can be added to regular trash, but recharge-able or button-type batteries should be recycled.

- Office supply stores will usually accept empty printer cartridges. They may also accept old electronic devices.

The average person in the United States uses about 250 liters (66 gallons) of water each day. By carefully conserving water using the ideas listed above, you and your family should be able to reduce your usage by at least 30 percent.

FACT

Most African farmers rely on rain to water their crops. A company known as KickStart International has devised a pump that can lift water from wells and provide enough pressure to irrigate two acres of land. Since most African farms have no electricity, the pumps operate by foot-power that the farmers provide. More than 65,000 of these pumps are now in operation.

By irrigating their crops, these farmers can plant and harvest valuable and much needed vegetables instead of grains.

Do Your Part to Make People Aware of the Need to Conserve Water

Be an advocate for water conservation and other green issues. Write letters or send e-mails to your councilman, mayor, congressman, and senators. Prepare posters that support water conservation. Speak out about water conservation and making America green in your classes and with your family and friends.

Glossary

acre-foot of water—The volume of water that covers an acre of land one foot (12 inches) deep. It equals 43,560 cubic feet (325,851 gallons) of water.

aquifer—An underground permeable and porous rock mass saturated with water.

boiling point—The temperature at which a liquid changes spontaneously from a liquid to a gas. At this temperature the pressure exerted by the liquid's vapor equals the pressure of the air.

capillarity—The tendency of water to "climb up" narrow glass tubes and other surfaces to which it adheres.

density—The ratio of mass to volume.

heat capacity—The heat needed to raise the temperature of a sample of matter by one degree Celsius.

ions—Atoms with a positive or negative charge. For example, sodium ions (Na^+) carry a positive charge; chloride ions (Cl^-) carry a negative charge.

irrigation—The artificial addition of water to agricultural crops.

low-flow faucets and showerheads, and low-flush toilets—Devices that reduce water flow and thus help to conserve water.

melting point—The temperature at which a solid changes to a liquid. It is the same as the freezing point, which is the temperature at which a liquid changes to a solid.

molecular mass—The relative mass of a molecule as compared to the mass of a carbon atom (formerly, an oxygen atom). The actual mass of the molecule can be found by dividing its molecular mass, expressed in grams, by 6×10^{23} (600 billion trillion).

negative electric charge—A rubber rod rubbed with fur has a negative charge. Anything repelled by a rubber rod rubbed with fur has a negative charge.

polar molecules—Molecules that are positively charged at one end and negatively charged the opposite end.

positive electric charge—A glass rod rubbed with silk has a positive charge. Anything repelled by a glass rod rubbed with silk has a positive charge.

solute—The substance that dissolves (disappears) in a solvent. For example, salt (the solute) dissolves in water (the solvent).

solvent—The substance in which a solute dissolves.

specific heat—The heat capacity of one gram of a substance.

surface tension—The skinlike quality of water. Water molecules are polar, so they attract one another, creating a cohesive (attractive) force that pulls them together. Molecules at water's surface are pulled inward, giving the surface of water a skinlike quality.

temperature—A measure of the average kinetic energy of molecules.

transpiration—The loss of water by evaporation from plants.

virtual water—The quantity of water needed to produce a product.

virtual water footprint—The amount of water a person uses in a year. It includes all the water used to produce the food we eat, the clothes we wear, and other products that require water to make, as well as the water we consume for our health and hygiene.

water cycle—The path that water follows as it moves from Earth to the atmosphere and back to Earth.

Appendix:
Science Supply Companies

Arbor Scientific
P.O. Box 2750
Ann Arbor, MI 48106-2750
(800) 367-6695
www.arborsci.com

Carolina Biological Supply Co.
2700 York Road
Burlington, NC 27215-3398
(800) 334-5551
http://www.carolina.com

Connecticut Valley Biological
Supply Co., Inc.
82 Valley Road, Box 326
Southampton, MA 01073
(800) 628-7748
http://www.ctvalleybio.com

Delta Education
P.O. Box 3000
80 Northwest Blvd
Nashua, NH 03061-3000
(800) 258-1302
**customerservice@delta-
    education.com**

Edmund Scientific's Scientifics
60 Pearce Avenue
Tonawanda, NY 14150-6711
(800) 728-6999
http://www.scientificsonline.com

Educational Innovations, Inc.
362 Main Avenue
Norwalk, CT 06851
(888) 912-7474
http://www.teachersource.com

Fisher Science Education
4500 Turnberry
Hanover Park, IL 60133
(800) 955-1177
http://www.fisheredu.com

Frey Scientific
100 Paragon Parkway
Mansfield, OH 44903
(800) 225-3739
http://www.freyscientific.com

Nasco-Fort Atkinson
P.O. Box 901
Fort Atkinson, WI 53538-0901
(800) 558-9595
http://www.enasco.com

Nasco-Modesto
P.O. Box 3837
Modesto, CA 95352-3837
(800) 558-9595
http://www.enasco.com

Sargent-Welch/VWR Scientific
P.O. Box 5229
Buffalo Grove, IL 60089-5229
(800) SAR-GENT
http://www.SargentWelch.com

Science Kit & Boreal Laboratories
777 East Park Drive
P.O. Box 5003
Tonawanda, NY 14150
(800) 828-7777
http://sciencekit.com

**Wards Natural Science
    Establishment**
P.O. Box 92912
Rochester, NY 14692-9012
(800) 962-2660
http://www.wardsci.com

Further Reading

Bardhan-Quallen, Sudipta. *Championship Science Fair Projects: 100 Sure-to-Win Experiments.* New York: Sterling, 2005.

Cherry, Lynne, and Gary Braasch. *How We Know What We Know About Our Changing Climate: Scientists and Kids Explore Global Warming.* Nevada City, Calif.: Dawn Publications, 2008.

Jefferis, David. *Green Power: Eco-energy without Pollution.* New York: Crabtree Publishing Company, 2006.

Knight, Mary Jane. *Why Should I Turn Off the Tap?* Mankato, Minn.: Smart Apple Media, 2009.

McKay, Kim and Jenny Bonnin. *True Green Kids: 100 Things You Can Do to Save the Planet.* Washington, D.C.: National Geographic Society, 2008.

Rhadigan, Joe, and Rain Newcomb. *Prize-Winning Science Fair Projects for Curious Kids.* New York: Lark Books, 2004.

Sobha, Geeta. *Green Technology: Earth Friendly Innovations.* New York: Crabtree Publishing Company, 2008.

Strauss, Rochelle. *One Well: The Story of Water on Earth.* Tonawanda, N.Y.: Kids Can Press Ltd., 2007.

Woodward, John. *Climate Change.* New York: DK Publishing, 2008.

Internet Addresses

Be Waterwise.
<http://www.bewaterwise.com>

Water Experiments for Kids.
<http://www.carlsbadca.gov/water/
wdkds.html>

Water Footprint.
<http://www.waterfootprint.org>

Index

A
acid rain, 69–75
acre-foot of water, 40
Africa, 95, 120
algal blooms, 77–79
ammonia, 45
aquifers
    modeling, 76
    overview, 72–74
    pollution, fighting, 74–75, 119
    pumping, polluting, 80–82
    salt water intrusion, 83–86
    water volume in, 87–88

B
bath *vs.* shower, 114–115
bogs, 101
boiling point, determining, 41–42, 45
bromine, 45

C
California, 40
capillarity, surface tension and, 33–36, 89
carbon dioxide, 70
China, 19, 20, 40
chlorine, 45
cleaners, making, 117–119
comets, 61
compounds, polar *vs.* nonpolar, 38
condensation nuclei, 66
confined aquifers, 72
conservation of water
    bath *vs.* shower, 114–115
    benefits, 17
    consumption, 107–108, 120
    dietary changes, 17, 20, 23
    foods, importing, 19–20
    household, methods, 116–120
    how you can help, 121
    leaks, 109–113
Crater Lake, 95

D
dams, 99–101
density, changes in, 47–48, 83–86
detergents, 116, 117
drip irrigation, 17

E
Egypt, 40
electricity, generating, 16, 93, 100
Environmental Protection Agency (EPA),
    74
experiments, designing, 8–9

F
fens, 101
floods, 96, 99–103
fluorine, 45
fossil fuels, 69

G
glaciers, 95
global warming, 69
Great Lakes, 95
greenhouse gases, 69
groundwater, 72–74, 117
guard cells, 89, 90

H
hazardous wastes, materials, 116, 119
heat capacity, determining, 53–59
Hoover Dam, 100
hydrogen, 43
hydrogen chloride, 45
hydrogen sulfide, 45

I
ionic compounds, 37–39
irrigation, 17, 40, 73, 100, 120
Israel, 17

J
Japan, 20
Jordan, 19–20

K
kettle ponds, 95
kinetic energy, 43, 44

L
lakes, 93, 95
leach fields, 78
leaks, 109–113

M
marshes, 101

Mead (Lake), 100
melting point, determining, 43–45
mercury, 100–101
metric measurement, 18
mirex, 73–74
Mississippi River, 93, 95

N

nitric acid, 69
nitric oxide, 45
nitrogen, 45, 77–79
nitrogen dioxide, 69

O

Ogallala Aquifer, 74
oxygen, 43

P

peat, 101–102
pH, 70
phosphorus, 77–79
polarity, 25, 27–28, 37–39
pollution
    acid rain, 69–75
    aquifers, 80–82, 119
    fossil fuels, 69
    non-point (runoff), 73–75
    point-source, 73
    sources of, 24, 61, 116, 117, 119
    urbanization and, 102–103
    wastewater, 77–79

R

rainfall, 15, 66–71
rain gardens, 74–75
recycling, 119, 120
rivers, 93–99
roof gardens, 103

S

safety, 11
sand heat capacity, determining, 58–59
science fairs, 10
scientific method, 8–9
seawater, 12–13, 83–86
sediment deposition, 93–95
septic tanks, 78
shower, bath vs., 114–115
soil, salty, 40
solubility, 37–39
specific heat, determining, 53–57
state changes, 46–49
stomata, 89, 90

sulfur dioxide, 69
sulfuric acid, 69
surface tension
    capillarity and, 33–36, 89
    demonstrating, 29–32
suspensions, 39

T

temperature, kinetic energy and, 43–44
Teton Dam, 100
toilets, 113, 116, 118
transpiration, 89–92
trees, 36

U

urbanization, 102–103

V

variables, 9
velocity measurements, water flow, 96–99
virtual water
    food production, 21
    footprint, 20, 22–23
    overview, 18–21
volume measurements
    aquifers, 87–88
    gas to solid, 47–49
    solid to gas, 46
    water flow, 96–99

W

water
air temperature and, 59
    bottled, 119
    distribution of, 13–15
    flow, measuring, 96–99
    fresh, 13, 40, 83–86, 95
    mass, 43, 45
    measurement of generally, 18
    overview, 24–26
    turnover, 51–52
    uses of, 16–18, 20
    virtual, 18–23
water cycle, 60–65
watersheds, 93
water table, 72, 83
wells, 110
wetlands
    aquatic plants, animals in, 104–106
    overview, 101–102
    urbanization and, 102–103
wheat, 18–19